Dedicated to our parents.
Thank you for everything.

Contents

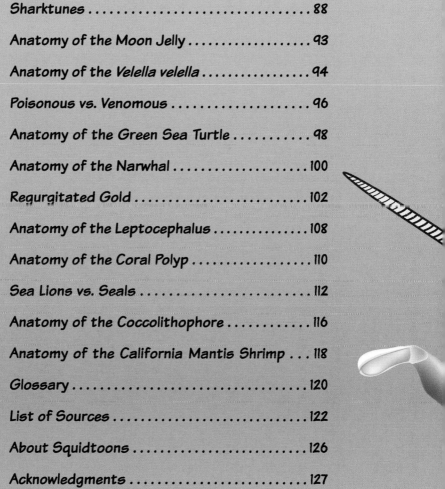

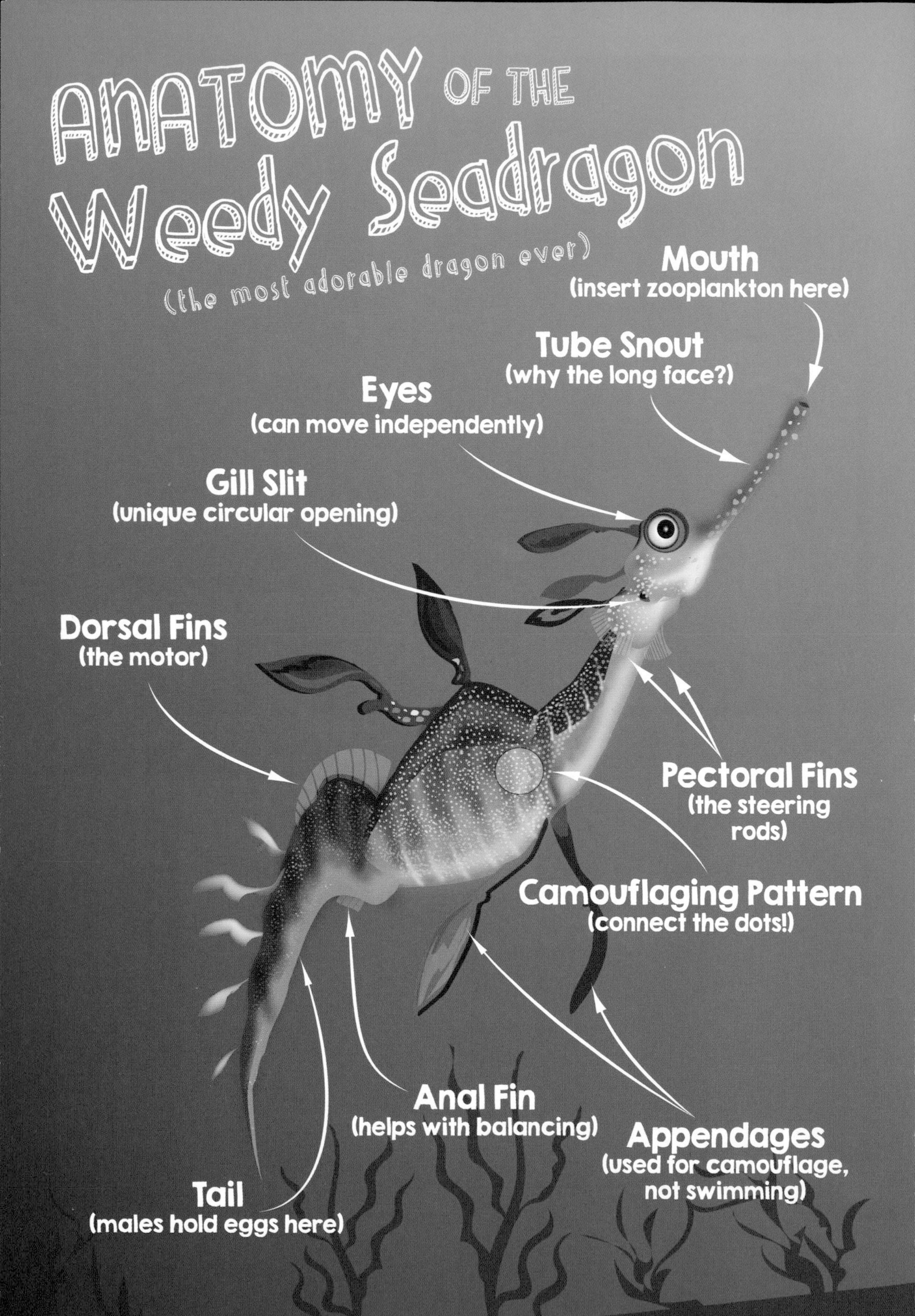

ANATOMY OF THE
Weedy Seadragon
(the most adorable dragon ever)
Mouth
(insert zooplankton here)
Tube Snout
(why the long face?)
Eyes
(can move independently)
Gill Slit
(unique circular opening)
Dorsal Fins
(the motor)
Pectoral Fins
(the steering rods)
Camouflaging Pattern
(connect the dots!)
Anal Fin
(helps with balancing)
Appendages
(used for camouflage, not swimming)
Tail
(males hold eggs here)

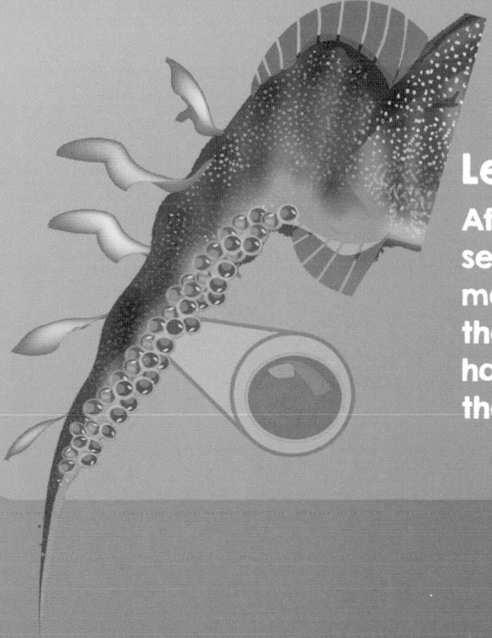

Leaving the Kids with Dad

After fertilization, the female seadragon attaches her eggs to the male seadragon's tail. Here, he guards them until they hatch. Once the babies hatch, they will swim away and forge their own paths.

Going with the Flow

Seadragons are poor swimmers, and they often drift in the current like uprooted seaweed. They also like to cling to clumps of seaweed and hunt for small crustaceans hiding in the foliage.

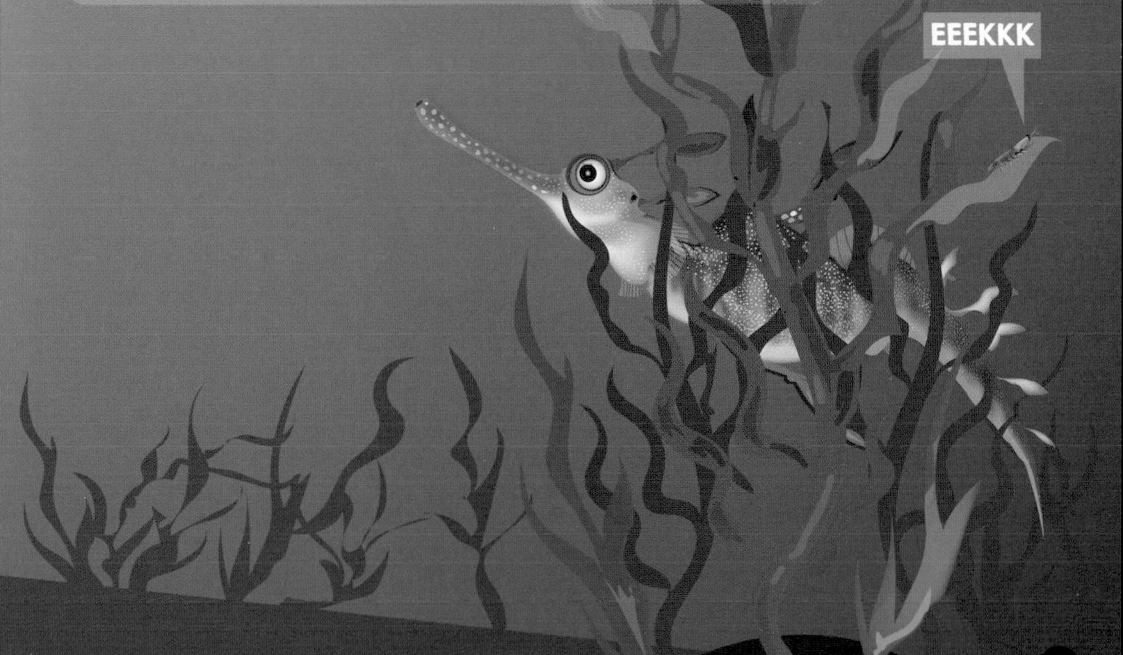
EEEKKK

SEADRAGONS

GIMME BABIES OR GIMME DEATH!

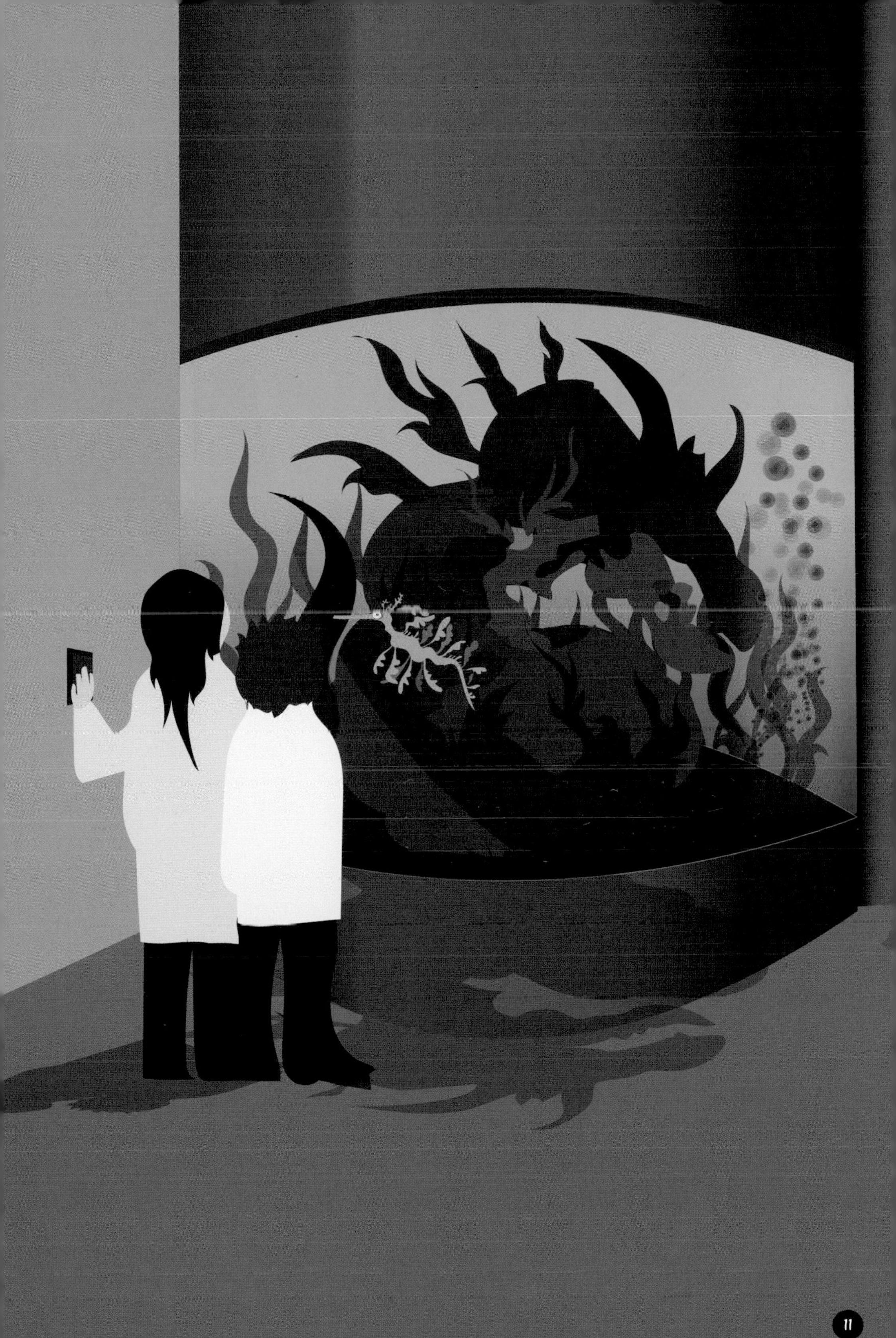

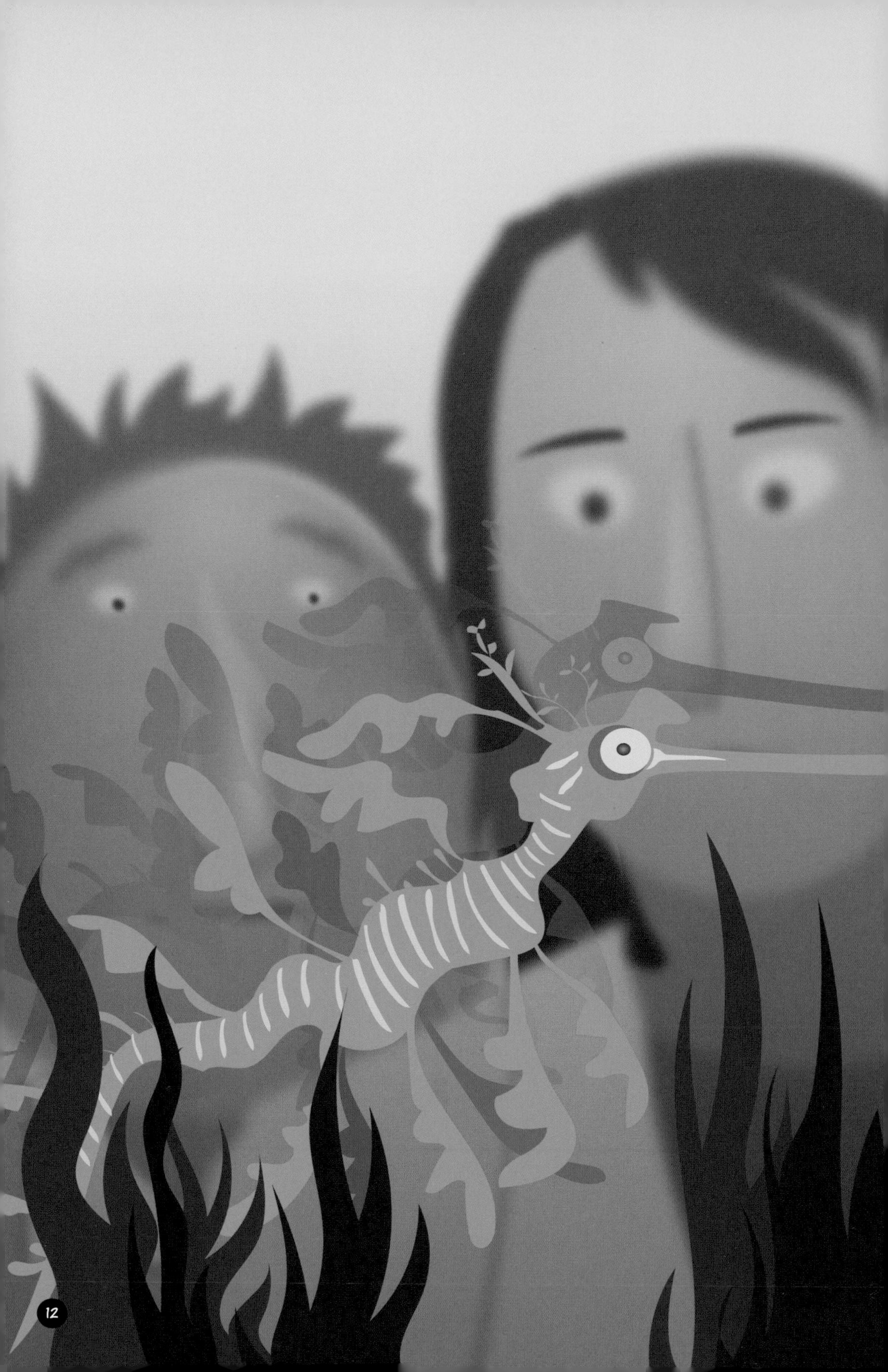

CURRENTLY, THERE ARE THREE SPECIES OF SEADRAGONS.

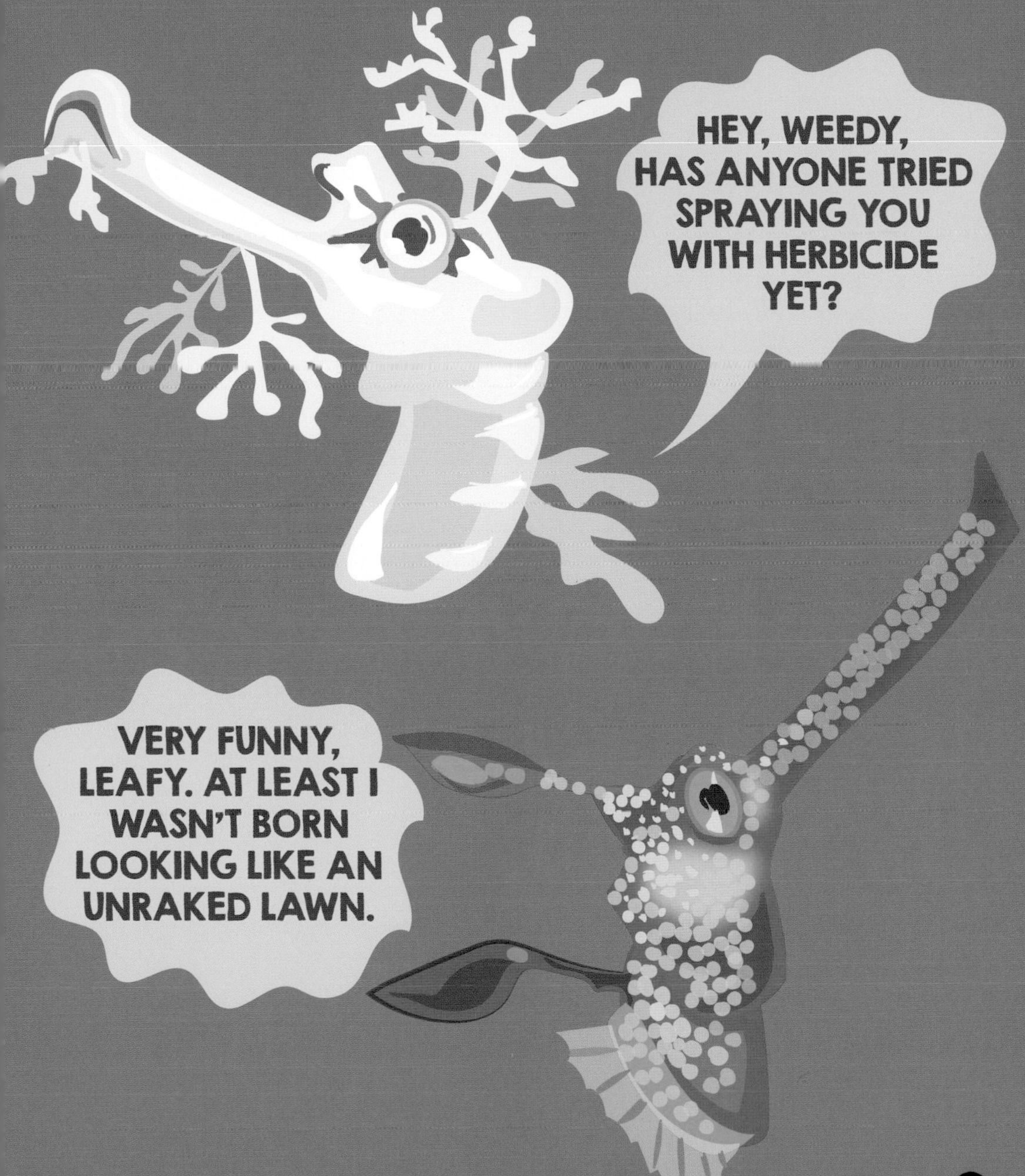
HEY, WEEDY, HAS ANYONE TRIED SPRAYING YOU WITH HERBICIDE YET?
VERY FUNNY, LEAFY. AT LEAST I WASN'T BORN LOOKING LIKE AN UNRAKED LAWN.

SEADRAGONS ARE NOT OVERSIZED, FIRE-BREATHING REPTILES OF THE DEEP.

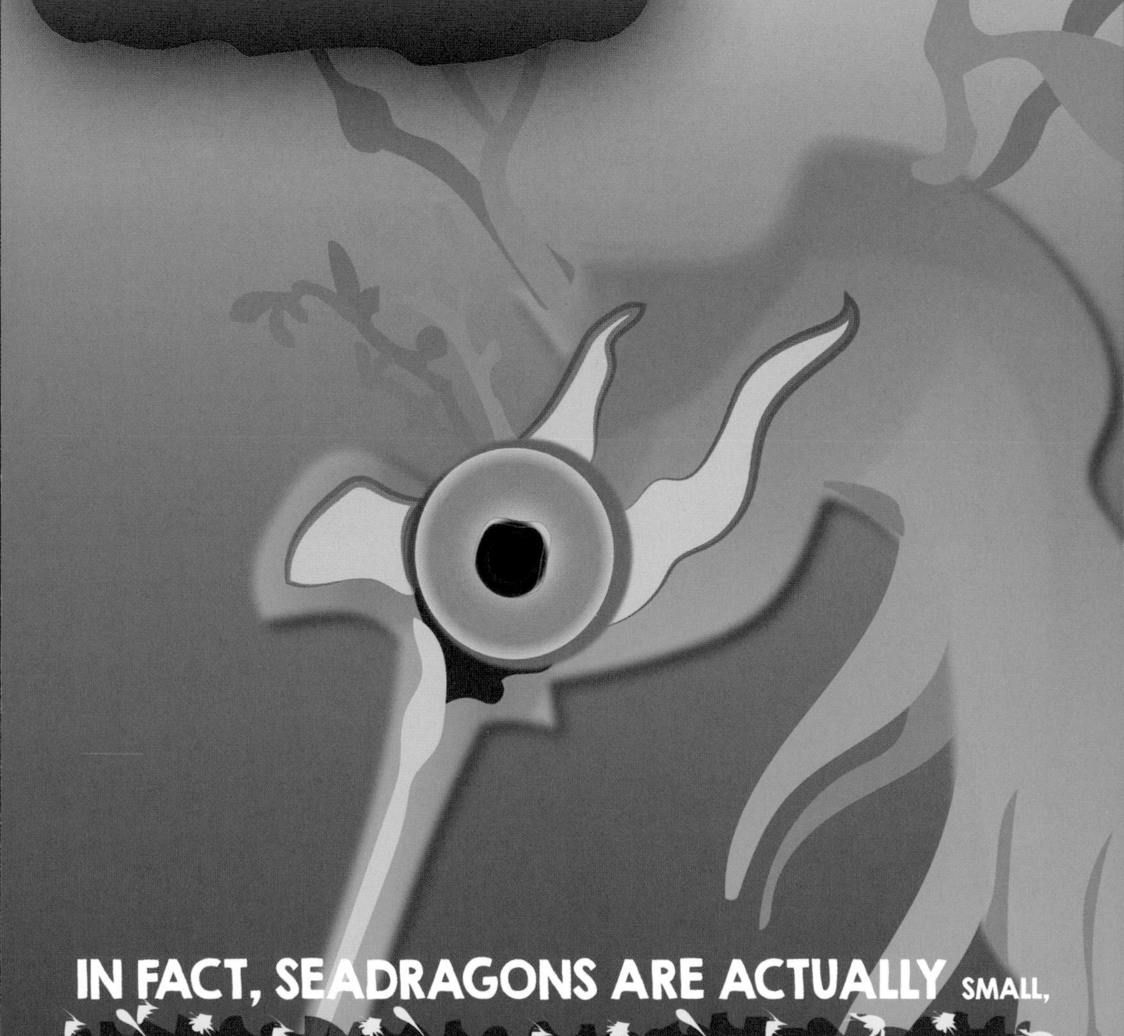

IN FACT, SEADRAGONS ARE ACTUALLY SMALL, PLANKTON-INHALING FISH OF RELATIVELY SHALLOW WATER.

DESPITE HAVING NO TEETH, SEADRAGONS ARE
CARNIVOROUS.

THEY SUSTAIN THEMSELVES BY SUCKING CRUSTACEANS INTO THEIR LONG, TUBULAR MOUTHS.

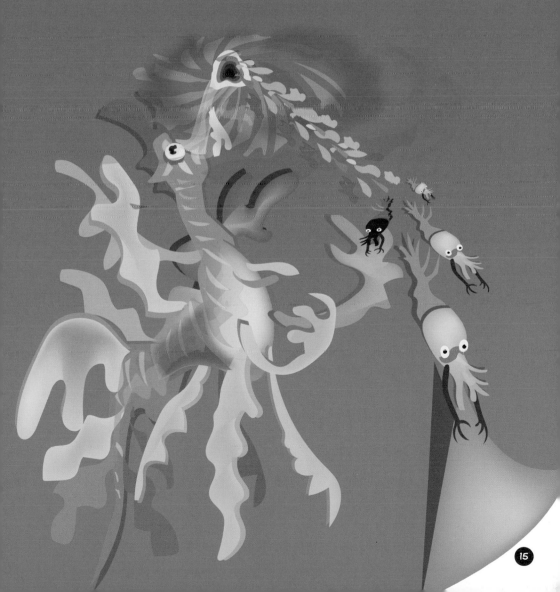

SEADRAGONS BELONG IN THE FAMILY SYNGNATHIDAE TOGETHER WITH SEAHORSES AND PIPEFISH.

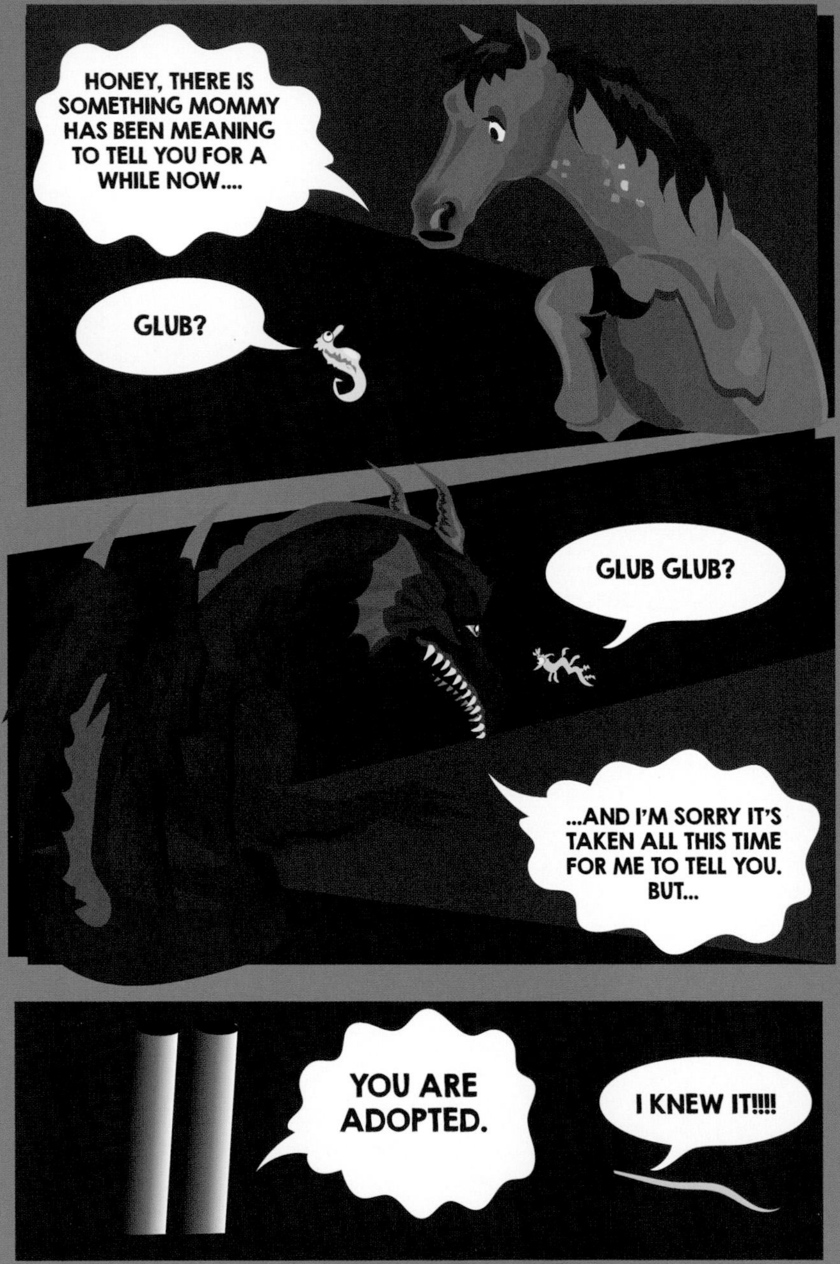
HONEY, THERE IS SOMETHING MOMMY HAS BEEN MEANING TO TELL YOU FOR A WHILE NOW....
GLUB?
GLUB GLUB?
...AND I'M SORRY IT'S TAKEN ALL THIS TIME FOR ME TO TELL YOU. BUT...
YOU ARE ADOPTED.
I KNEW IT!!!!

DESPITE THEIR NAMES AND APPEARANCE, SEADRAGONS, SEAHORSES, AND PIPEFISH ARE ALL FISH!

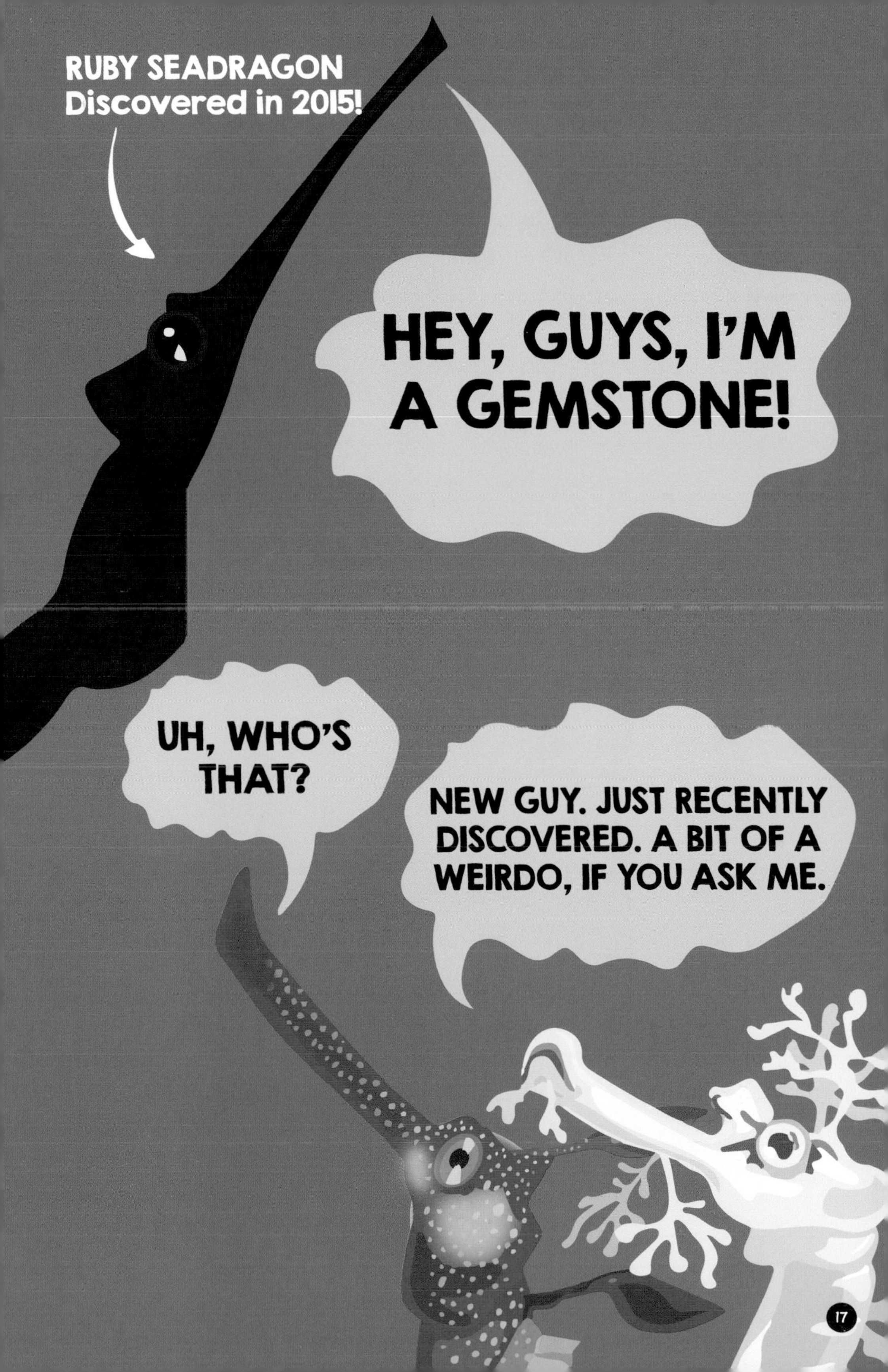
RUBY SEADRAGON
Discovered in 2015!
HEY, GUYS, I'M A GEMSTONE!
UH, WHO'S THAT?
NEW GUY. JUST RECENTLY DISCOVERED. A BIT OF A WEIRDO, IF YOU ASK ME.

LEAFIES ARE CHARACTERIZED BY THEIR NUMEROUS LEAFY APPENDAGES, WHICH ALLOW THEM TO BLEND IN EFFORTLESSLY AMONG SEAWEED.

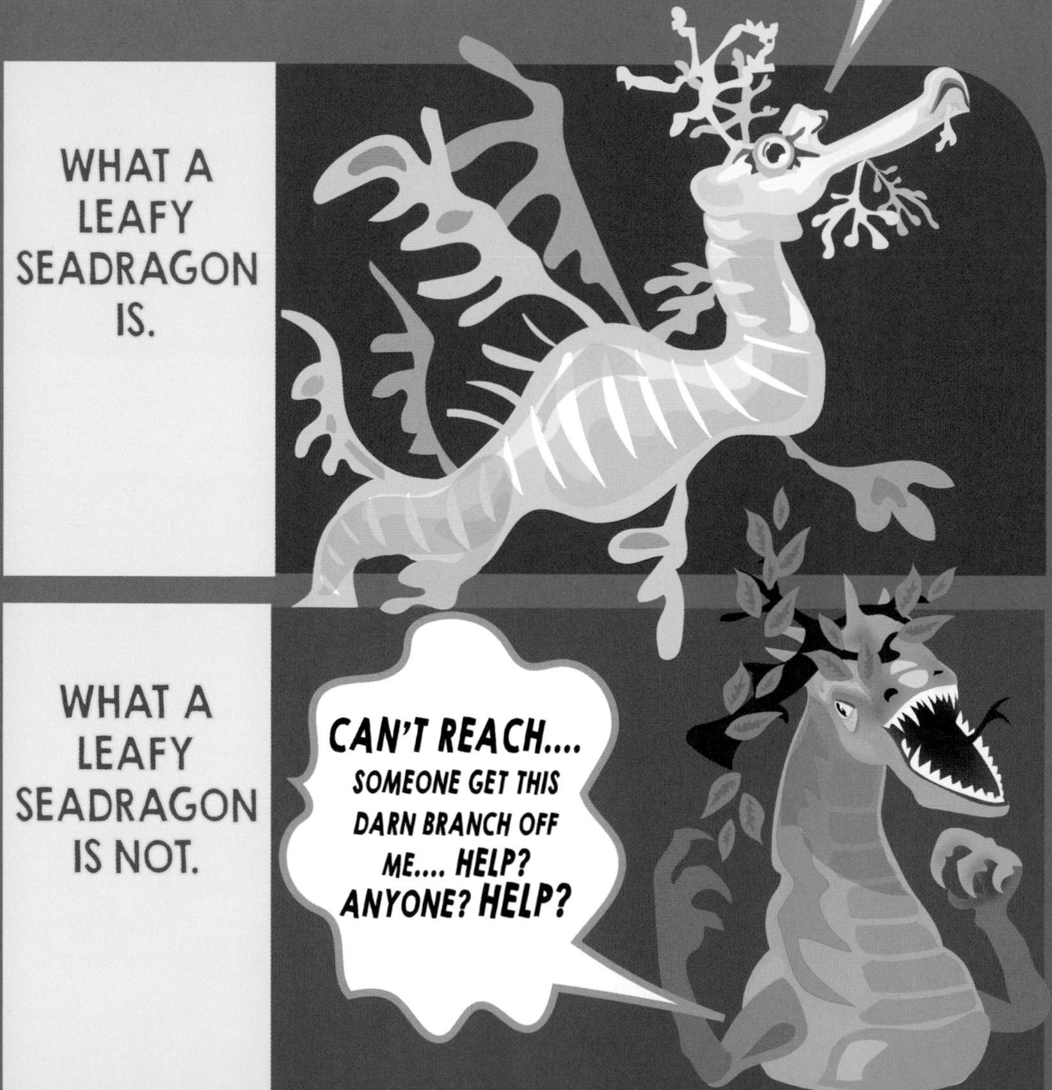
I'M THE REAL DEAL, GUYS.
WHAT A LEAFY SEADRAGON IS.
WHAT A LEAFY SEADRAGON IS NOT.
CAN'T REACH.... SOMEONE GET THIS DARN BRANCH OFF ME.... HELP? ANYONE? HELP?

WEEDIES, IN CONTRAST TO THEIR LEAFY COUNTERPART, RELY ON THEIR DISRUPTIVE COLOR PATTERNS, MUCH LIKE THOSE OF AN ARMY UNIFORM.

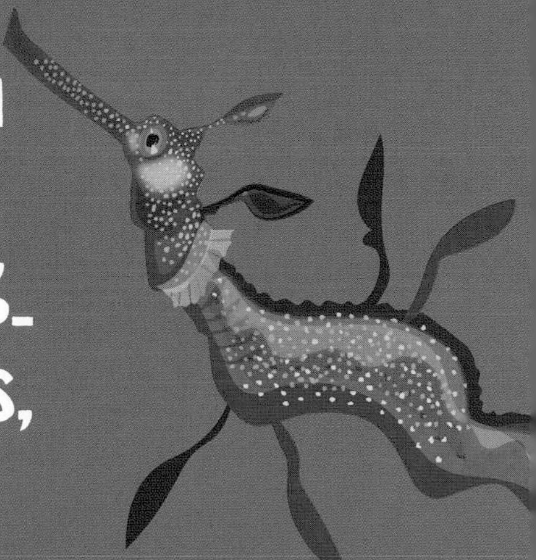

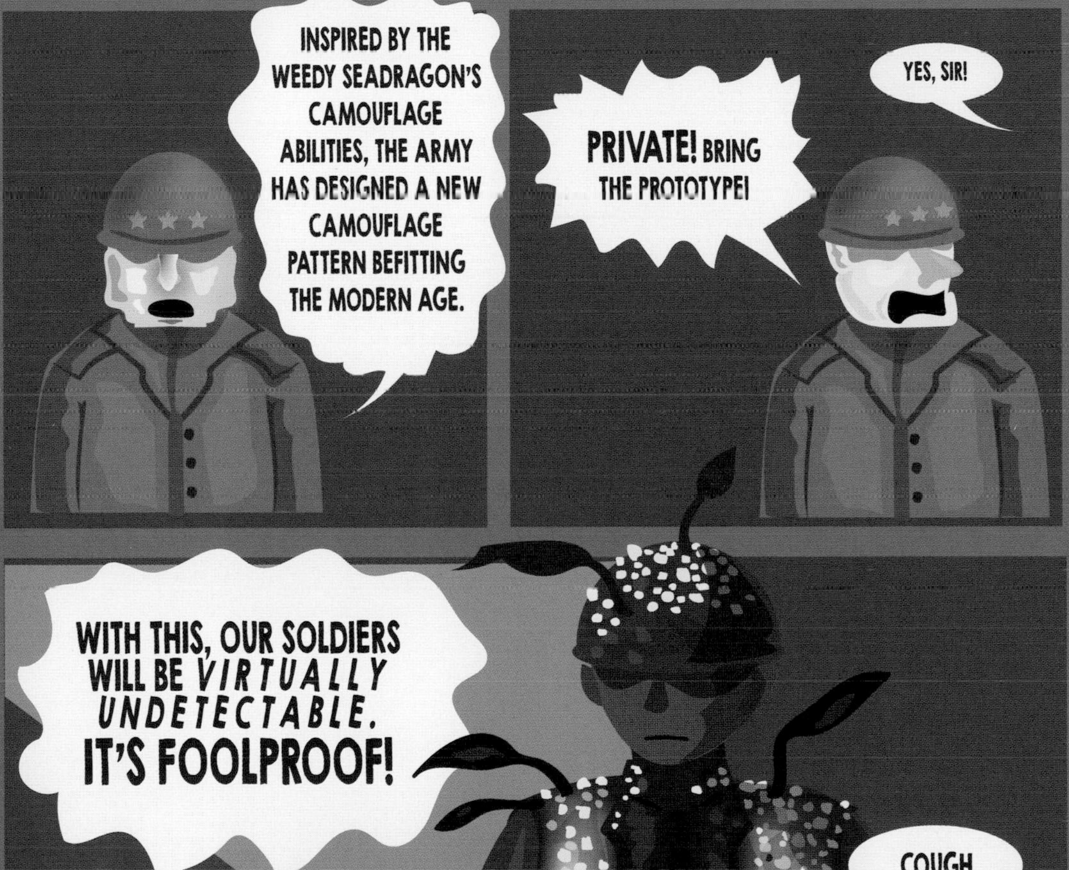
INSPIRED BY THE WEEDY SEADRAGON'S CAMOUFLAGE ABILITIES, THE ARMY HAS DESIGNED A NEW CAMOUFLAGE PATTERN BEFITTING THE MODERN AGE.
PRIVATE! BRING THE PROTOTYPE!
YES, SIR!
WITH THIS, OUR SOLDIERS WILL BE *VIRTUALLY UNDETECTABLE.* IT'S FOOLPROOF!
COUGH
WHAT WAS THAT, PRIVATE?
N-NOTHING, SIR.

RUBIES ARE STILL AN ENIGMA, AS THEY WERE JUST RECENTLY DISCOVERED. WHAT'S CERTAIN, HOWEVER, IS THAT THEY'RE QUITE RED AND VERY PRETTY.

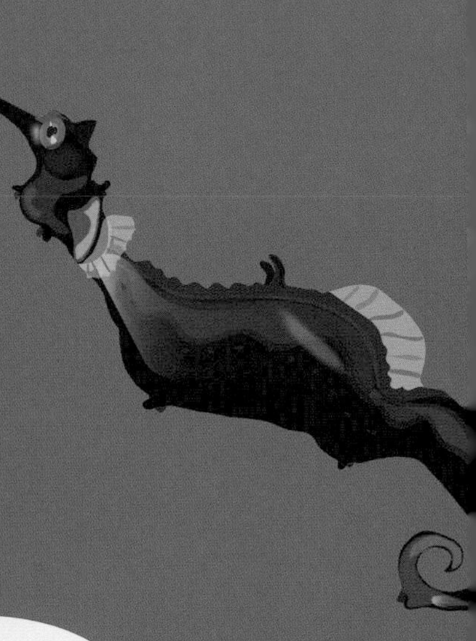

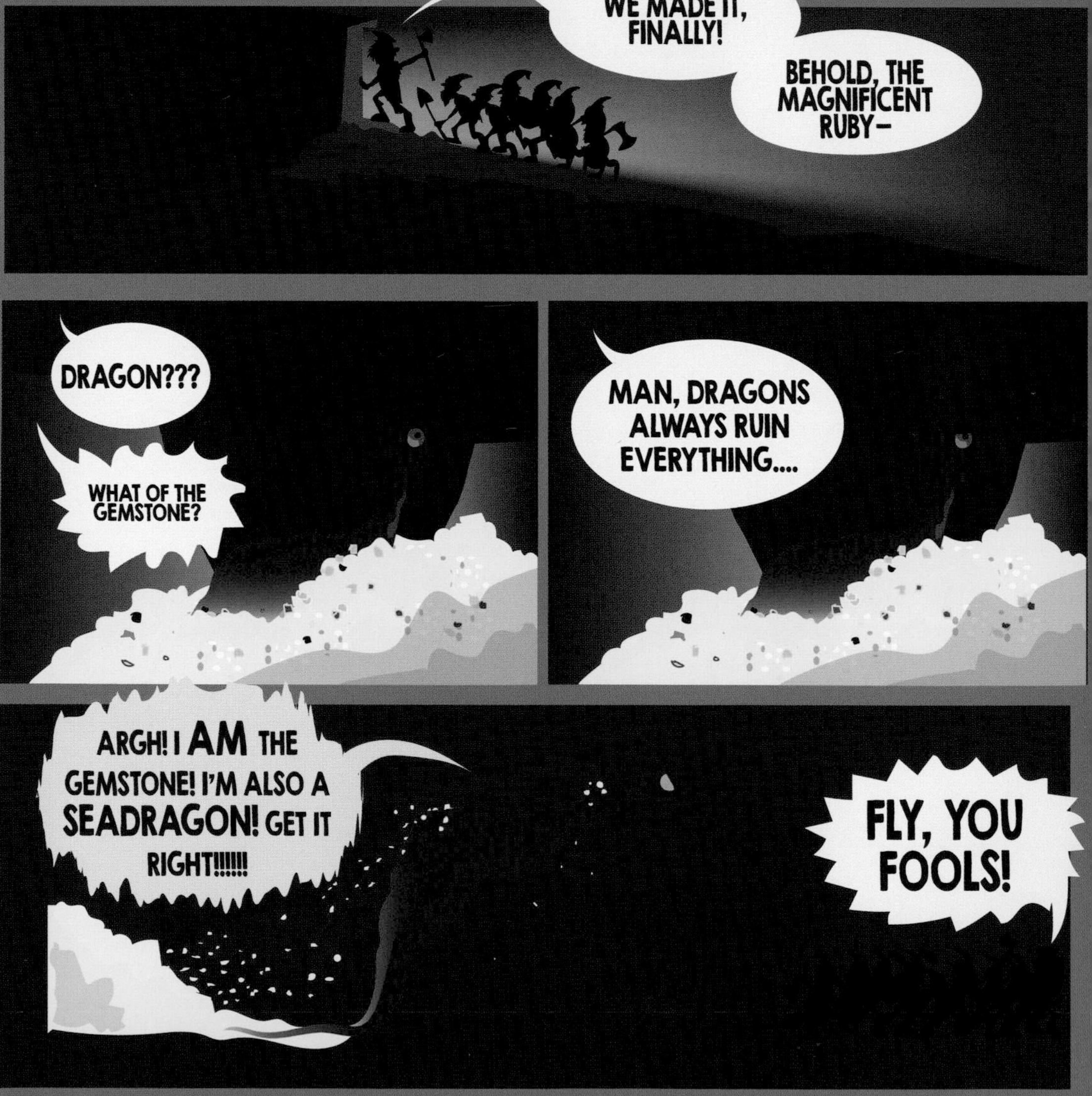
WE MADE IT, FINALLY!
BEHOLD, THE MAGNIFICENT RUBY—
DRAGON???
WHAT OF THE GEMSTONE?
MAN, DRAGONS ALWAYS RUIN EVERYTHING....
ARGH! I AM THE GEMSTONE! I'M ALSO A SEADRAGON! GET IT RIGHT!!!!!!
FLY, YOU FOOLS!

SEADRAGONS ARE ENDEMIC (ONLY FOUND IN A CERTAIN REGION) TO SOUTHERN AUSTRALIA'S OCEAN.

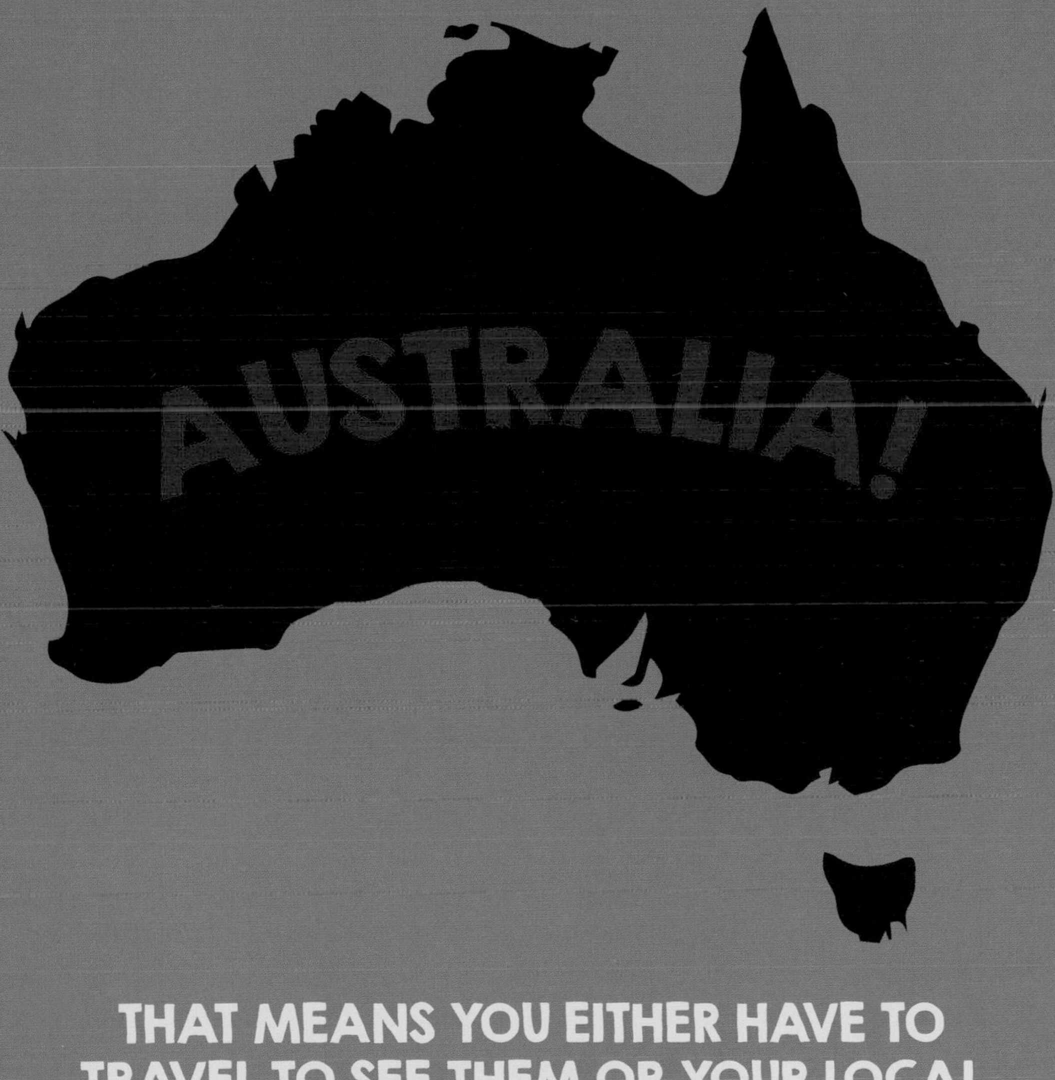
AUSTRALIA!

THAT MEANS YOU EITHER HAVE TO TRAVEL TO SEE THEM OR YOUR LOCAL AQUARIUM WOULD HAVE TO LEARN HOW TO RAISE, KEEP, AND BREED THEM.

BECAUSE THERE IS LITTLE RESEARCH DONE ON THE SEADRAGONS, AQUARISTS HAVE TO START AT SQUARE ONE. ONE BIG CHALLENGE IS TO STUDY THEIR

MATING HABITS.

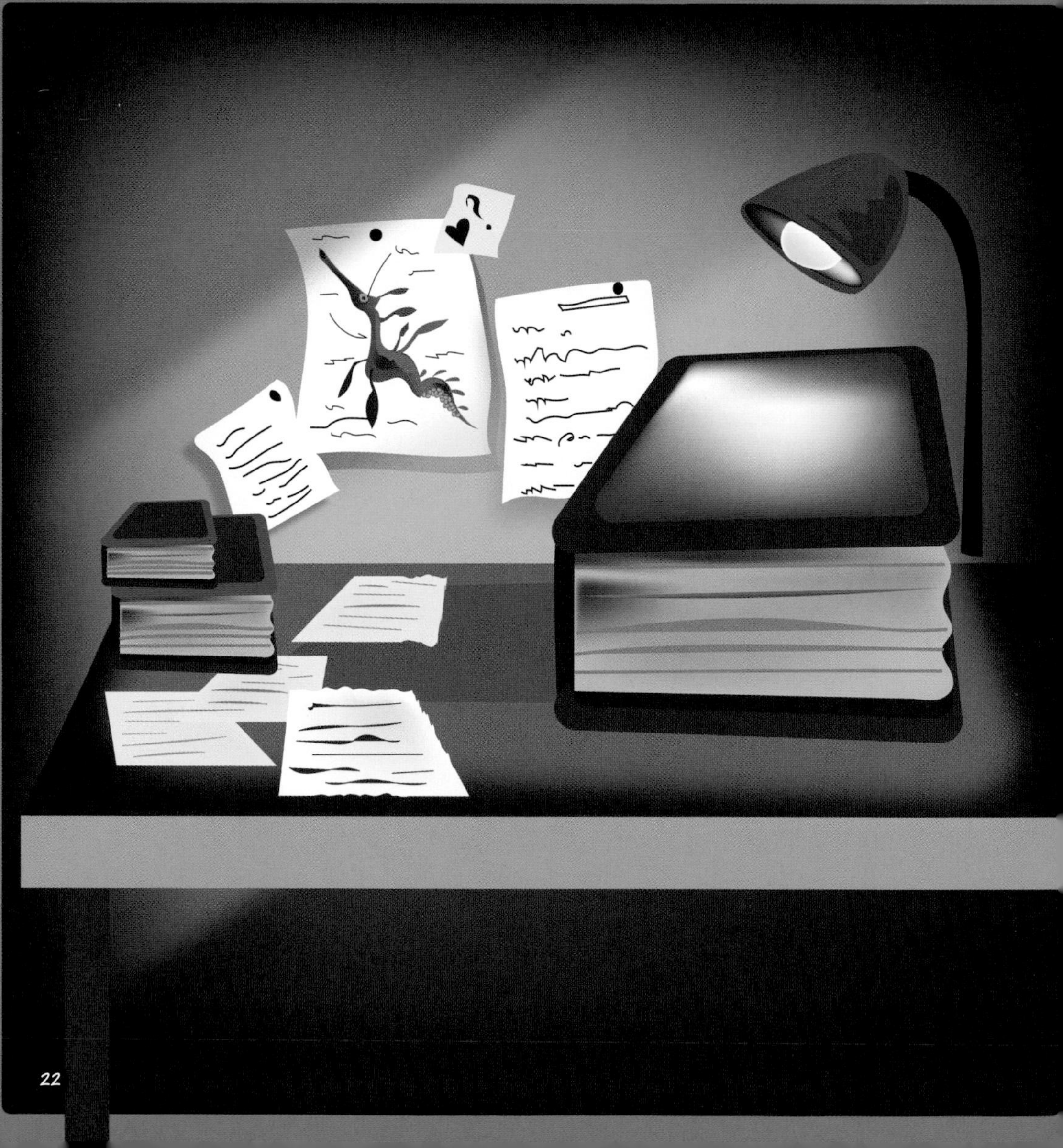

MATING AND SUCCESSFUL BIRTH OF BABIES HAVE ALWAYS BEEN INDICATORS OF A ZOO'S OR AQUARIUM'S SUCCESS IN PROVIDING A COMFORTABLE HOME.

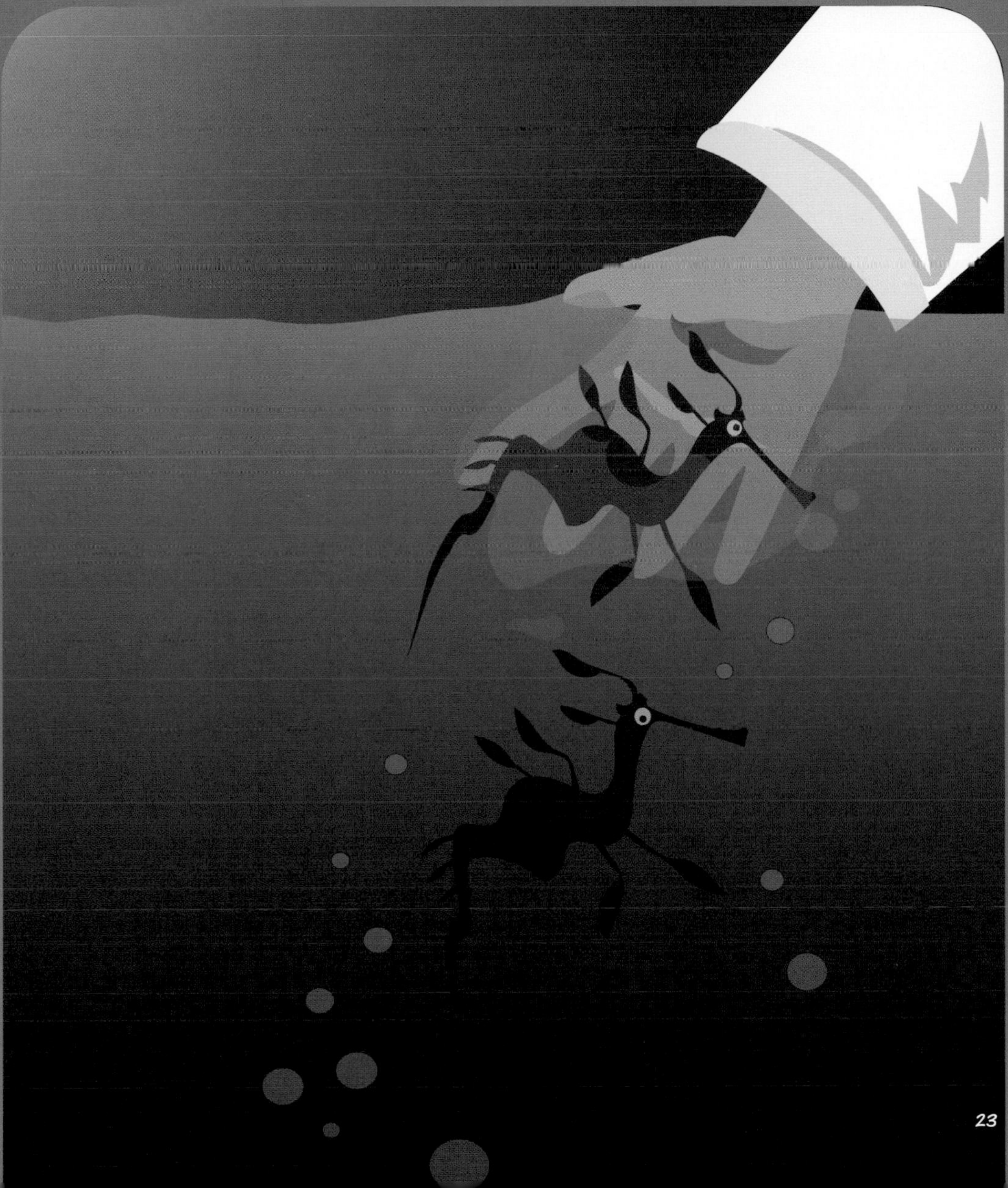

ALTHOUGH A FEW AQUARIUMS
HAVE SUCCESSFULLY HATCHED
SEADRAGON BABIES, ALL BIRTHS
HAVE OCCURRED SPONTANEOUSLY
AND INCONSISTENTLY.

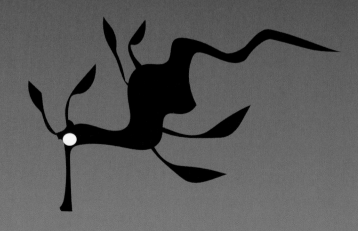

THIS MEANS THAT WE STILL CANNOT REPLICATE THE BREEDING PROCESS...

...WHICH MEANS FEWER SEADRAGON BABIES TO GO AROUND....

SO WHAT MIGHT BE THE PROBLEM?

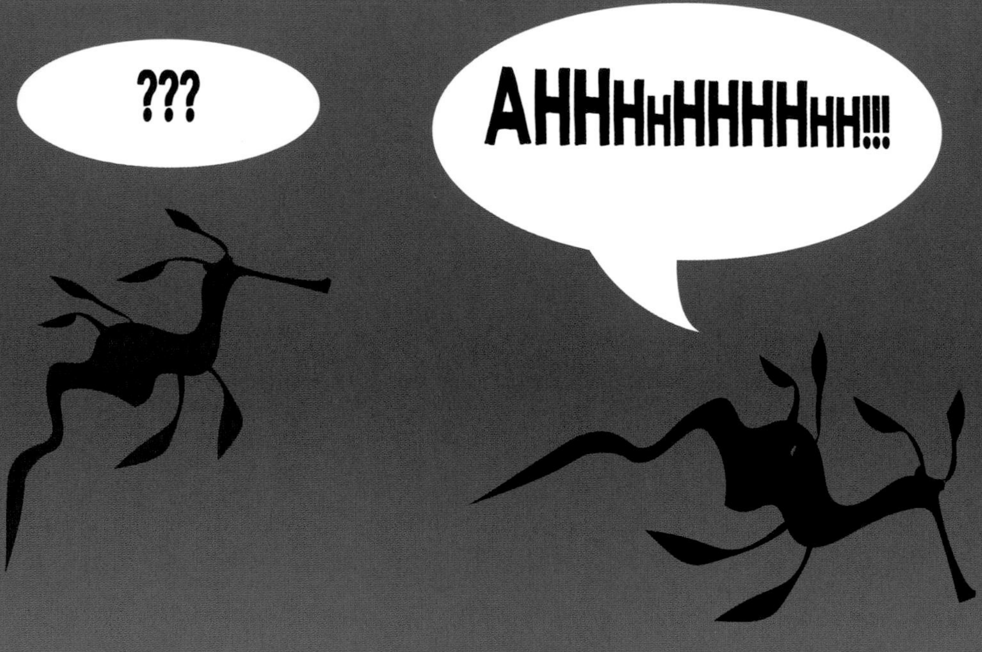
???
AHHHhHHHHhh!!!

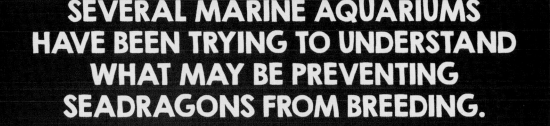

SEVERAL MARINE AQUARIUMS HAVE BEEN TRYING TO UNDERSTAND WHAT MAY BE PREVENTING SEADRAGONS FROM BREEDING.

MUFFLING AQUARIUM AMBIENCE

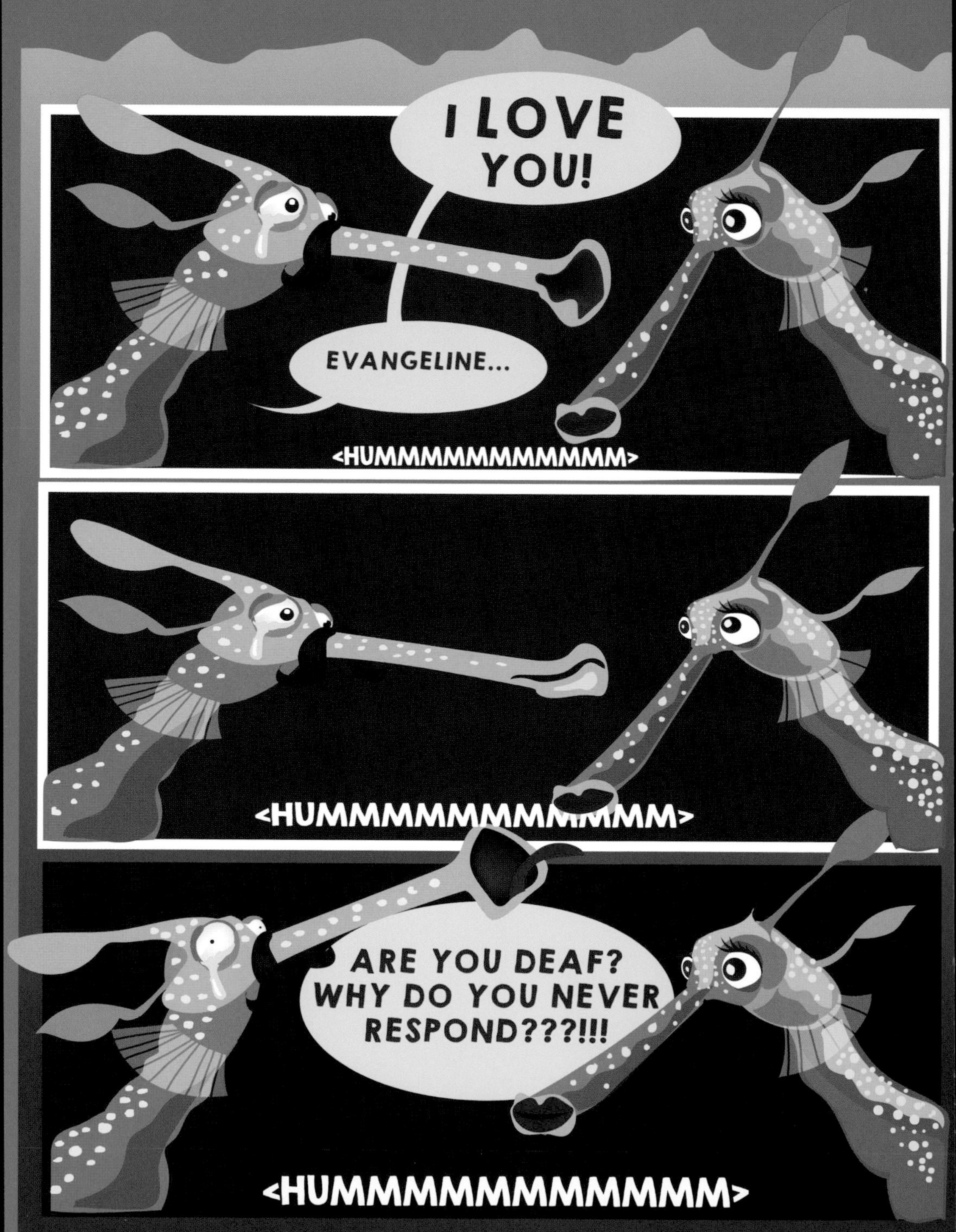
EVANGELINE...
I LOVE YOU!
<HUMMMMMMMMMMM>
<HUMMMMMMMMMMM>
ARE YOU DEAF? WHY DO YOU NEVER RESPOND???!!!
<HUMMMMMMMMMM>

MIMICKING NATURAL LIGHT SETTINGS

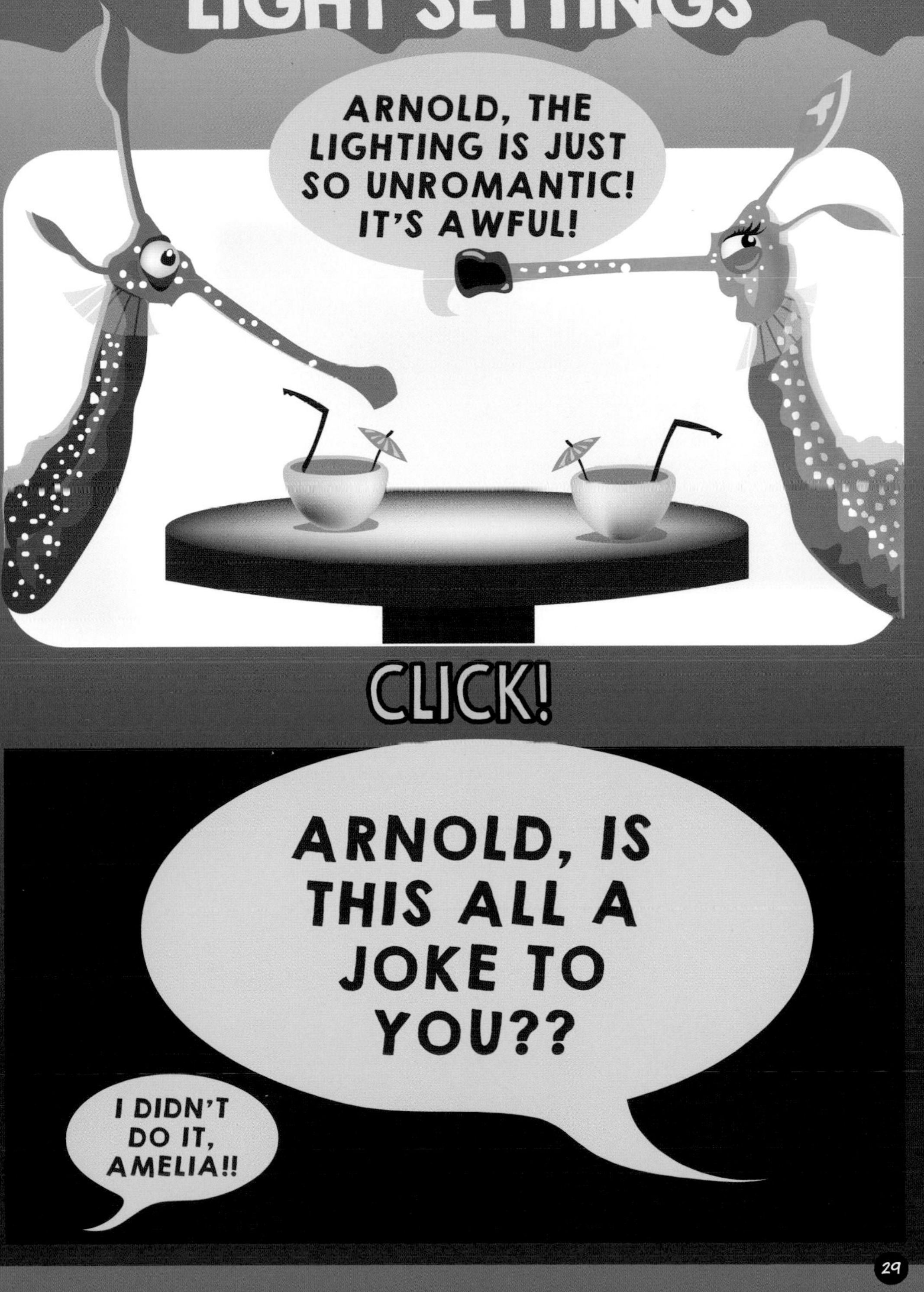

INCREASING TANK WIDTH AND HEIGHT

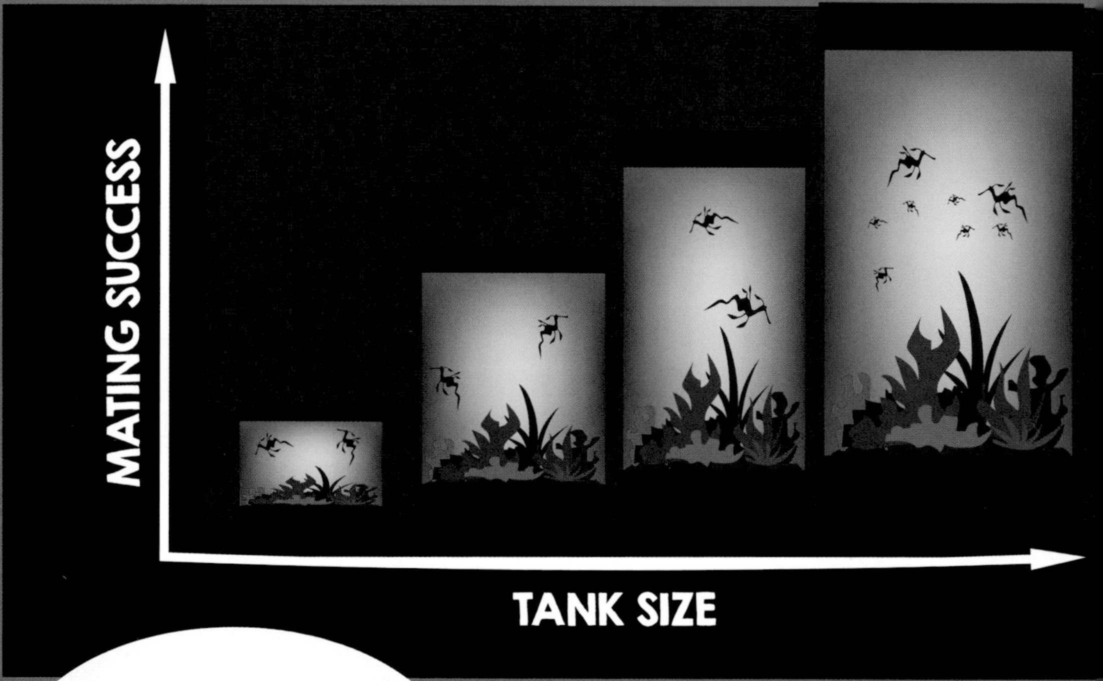
MATING SUCCESS
TANK SIZE

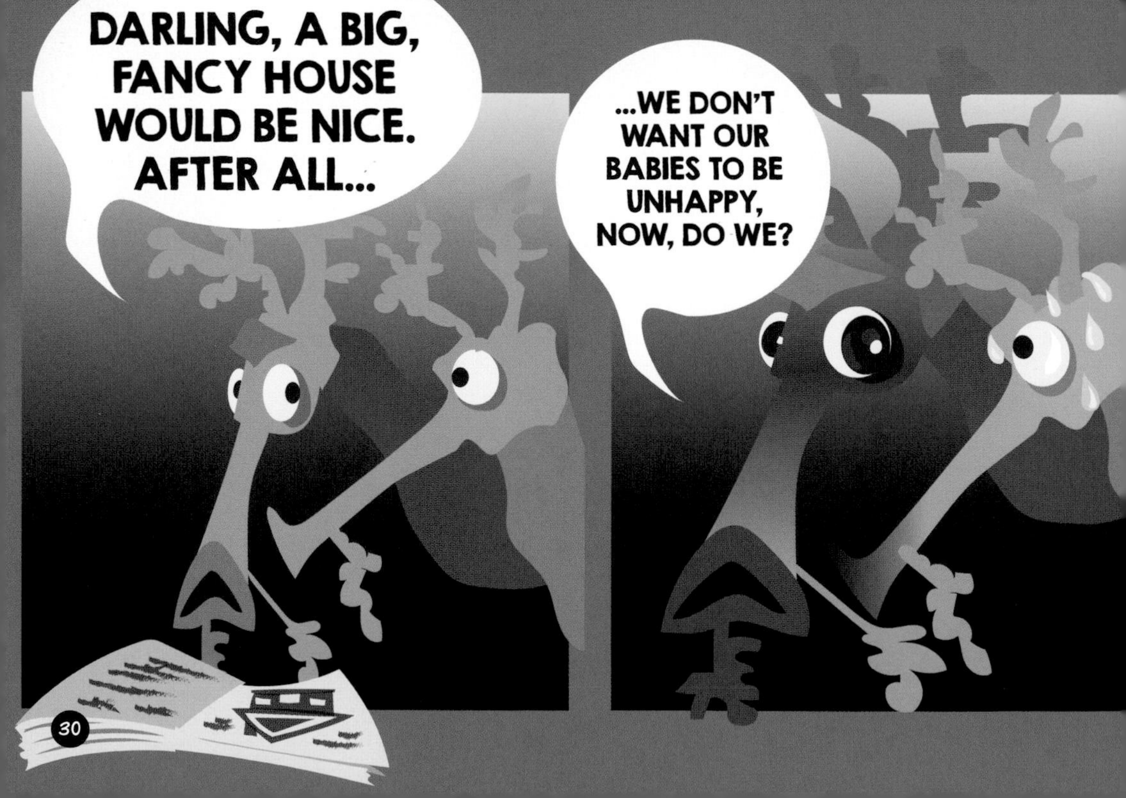
DARLING, A BIG, FANCY HOUSE WOULD BE NICE. AFTER ALL...
...WE DON'T WANT OUR BABIES TO BE UNHAPPY, NOW, DO WE?

ENHANCE THE SELECTION OF FOOD

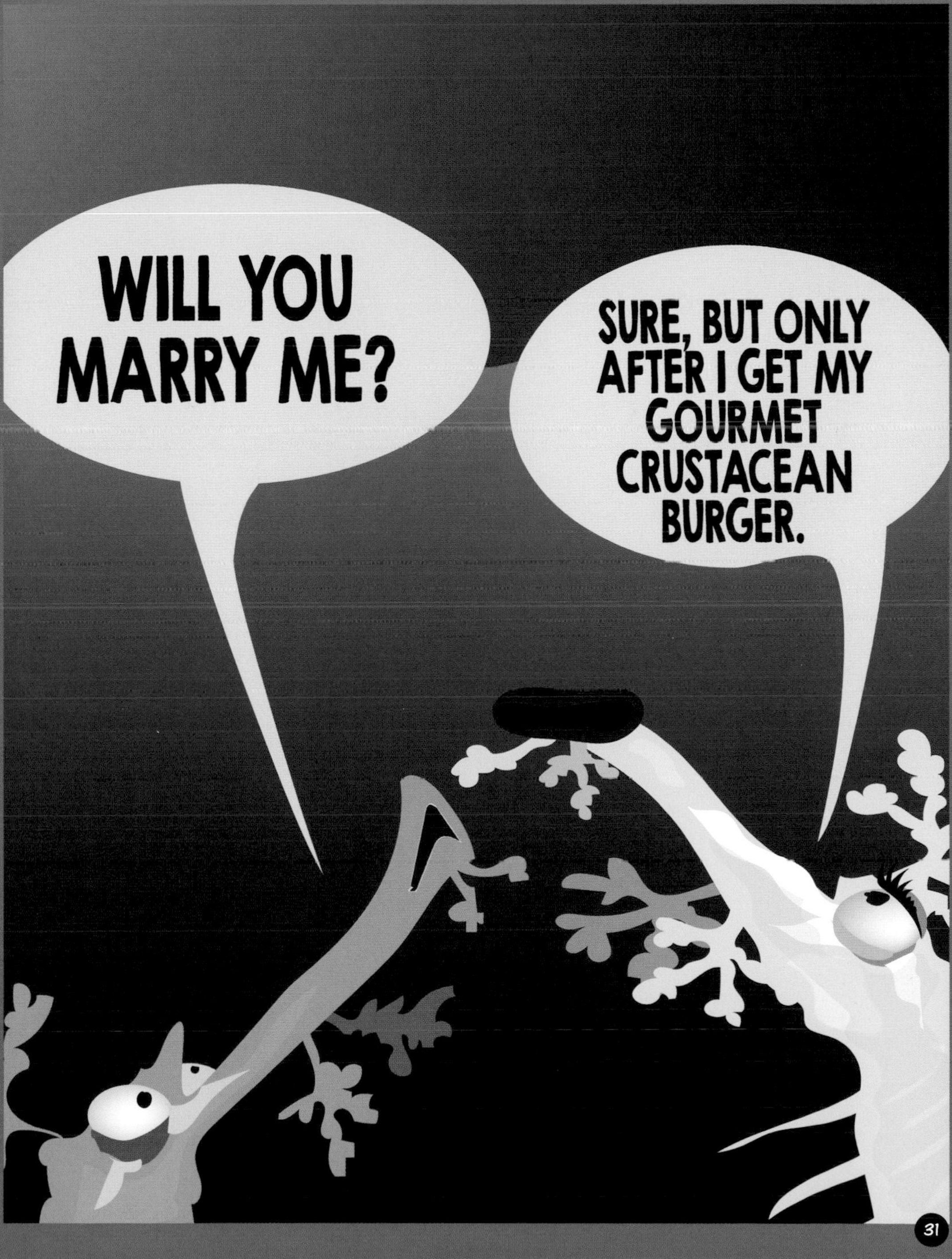
WILL YOU MARRY ME?
SURE, BUT ONLY AFTER I GET MY GOURMET CRUSTACEAN BURGER.

MIMICKING THE MOON CYCLE AND SEASONAL CHANGES

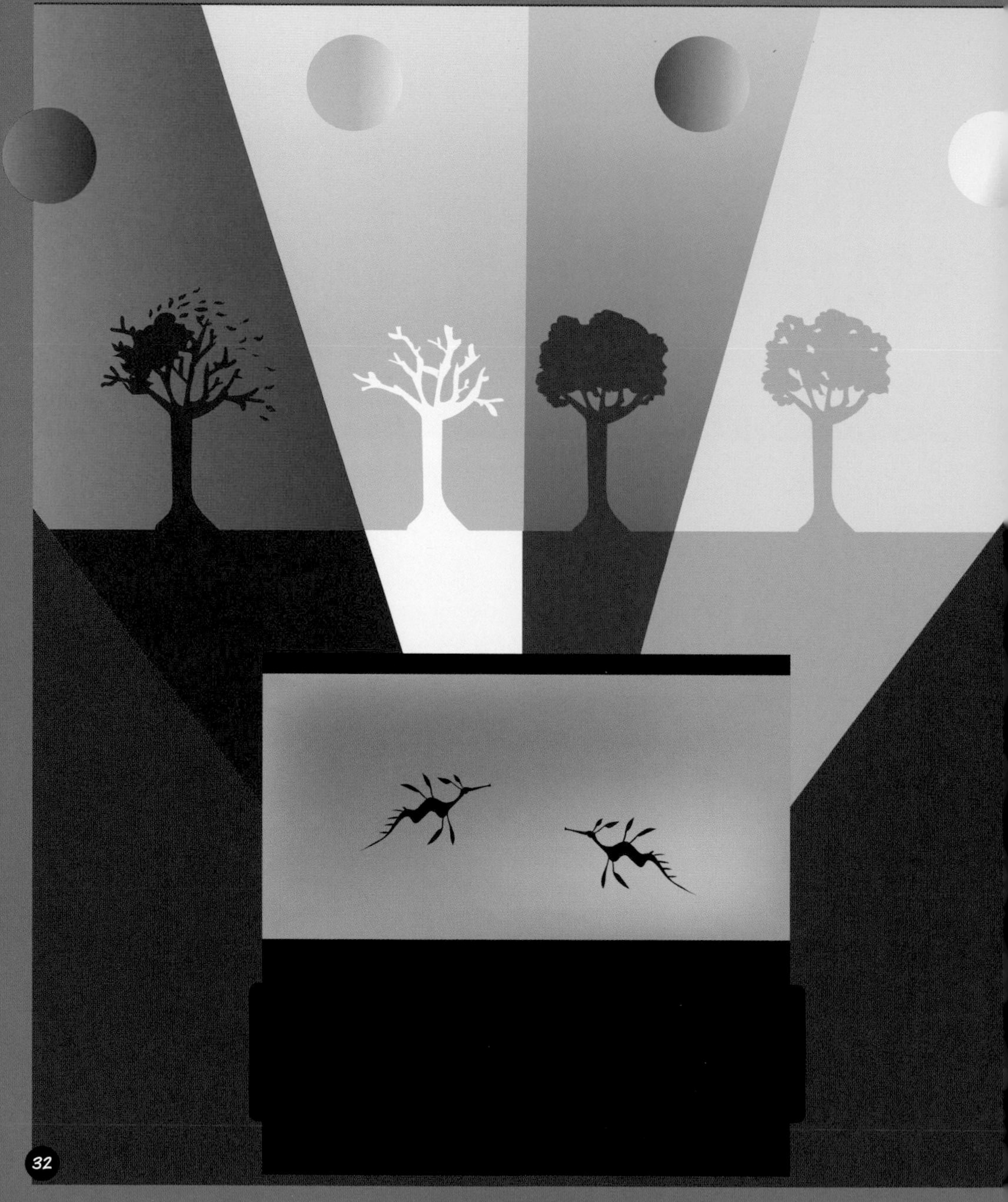

TO DOCUMENT EVERYTHING, SOME AQUARIUMS HAVE SET UP HD CAMERAS TO RECORD THE SEADRAGONS' ACTIVITIES 24-7.
HONEY, I HAVE A FEELING WE ARE BEING WATCHED....

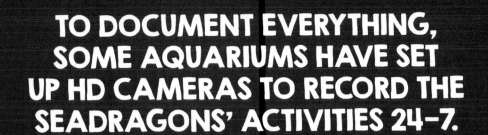

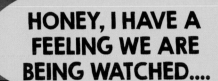

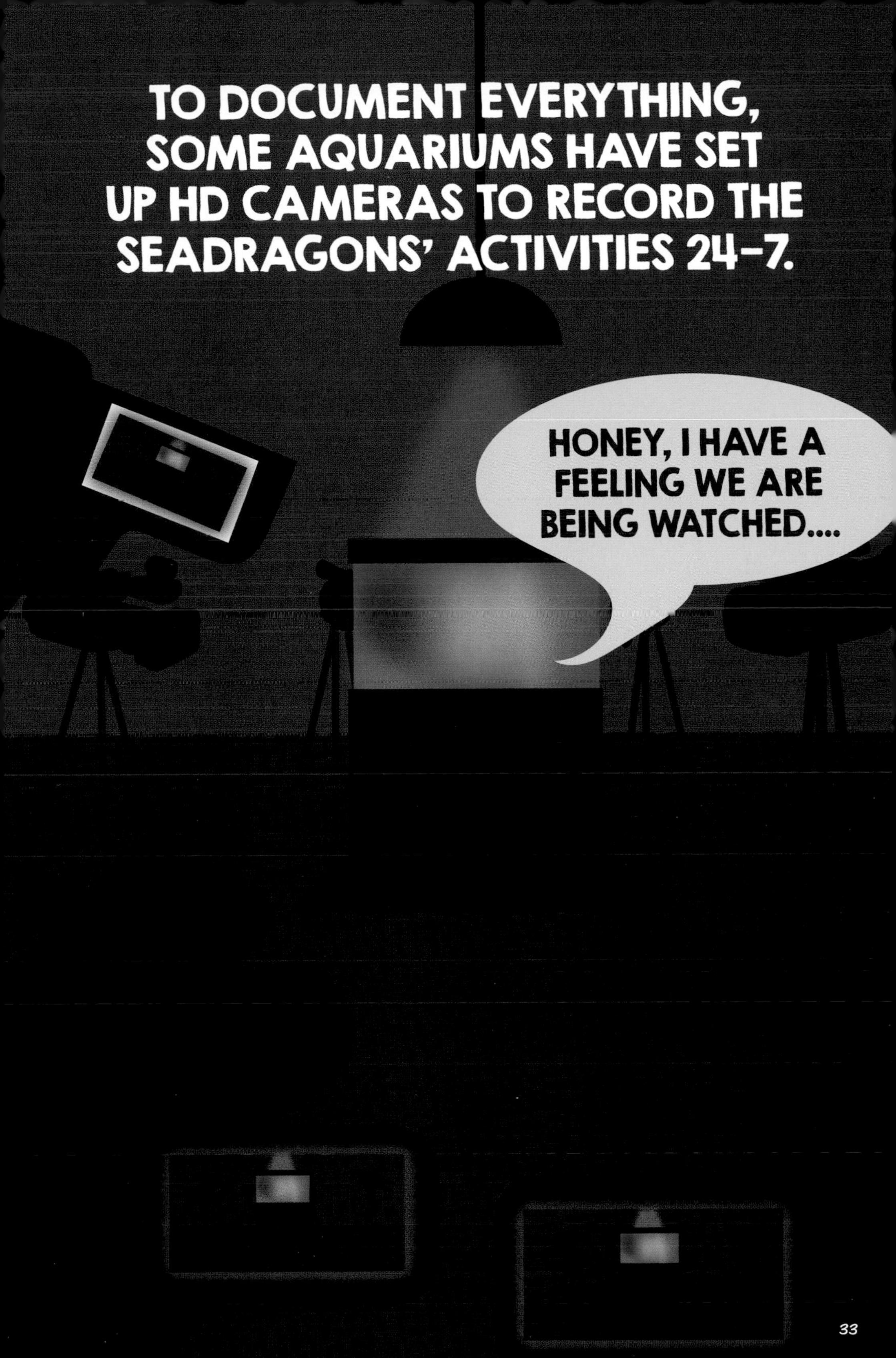

SO WHY ARE ALL THESE MEASURES NECESSARY?

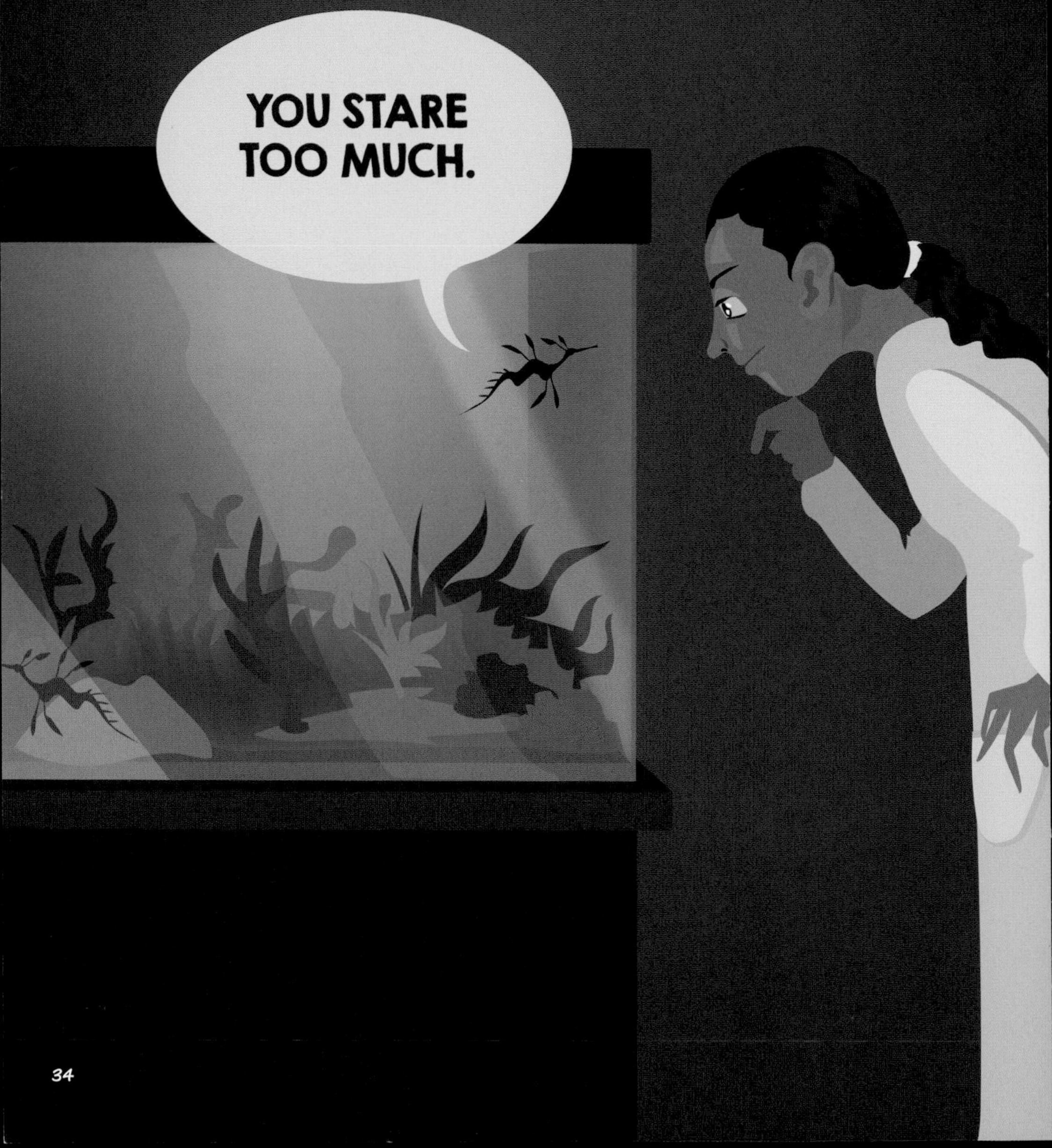
YOU STARE TOO MUCH.

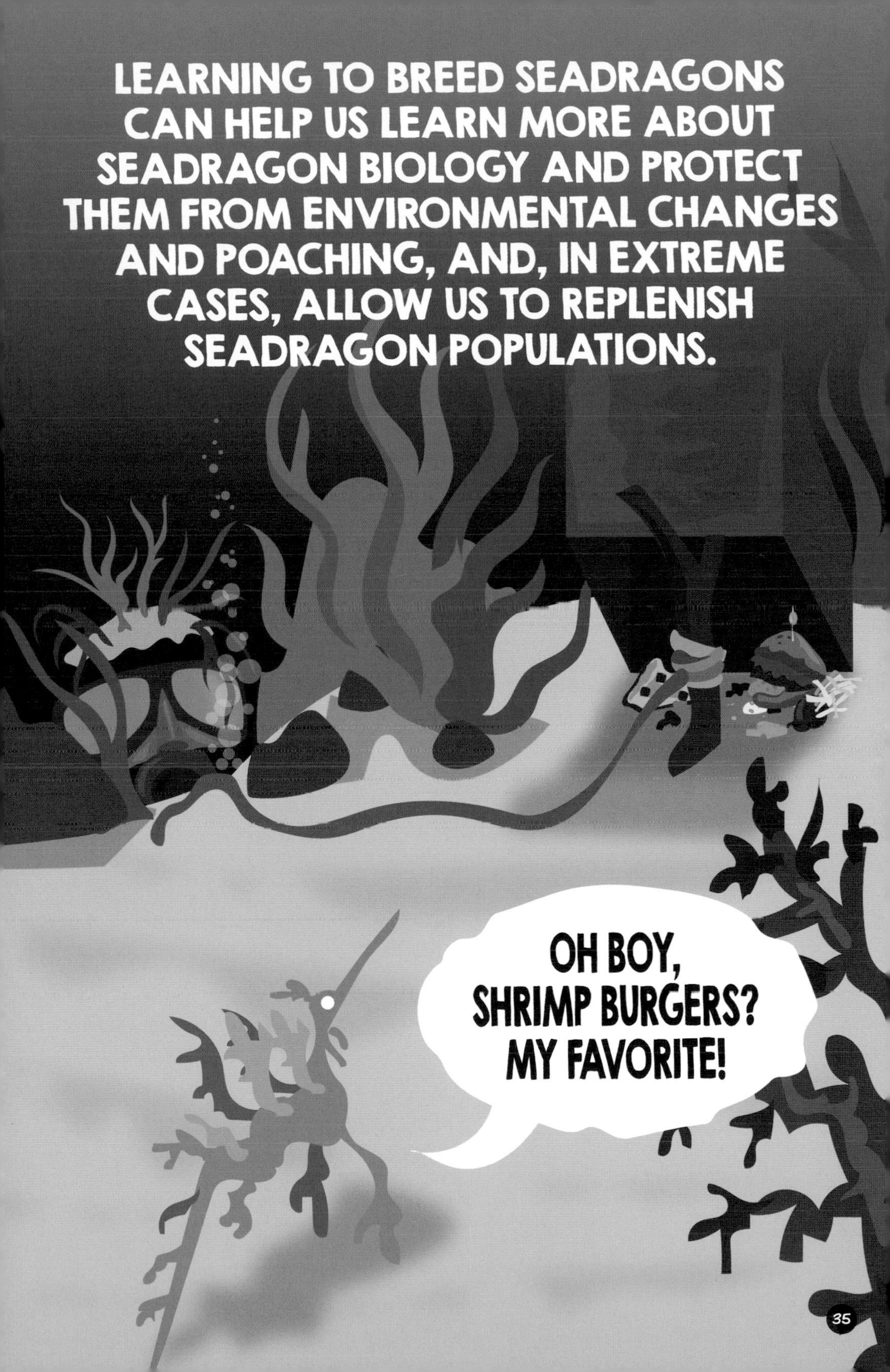
LEARNING TO BREED SEADRAGONS CAN HELP US LEARN MORE ABOUT SEADRAGON BIOLOGY AND PROTECT THEM FROM ENVIRONMENTAL CHANGES AND POACHING, AND, IN EXTREME CASES, ALLOW US TO REPLENISH SEADRAGON POPULATIONS.
OH BOY, SHRIMP BURGERS? MY FAVORITE!

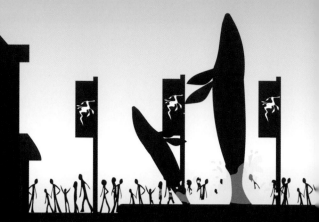

BUT MORE IMPORTANTLY, HAVING
SEADRAGONS AT AQUARIUMS WILL
PROVIDE A MORE AFFORDABLE OPTION
FOR THE PUBLIC TO MEET A PECULIAR
AMBASSADOR FROM THE SEA...

A LIVE SEADRAGON.

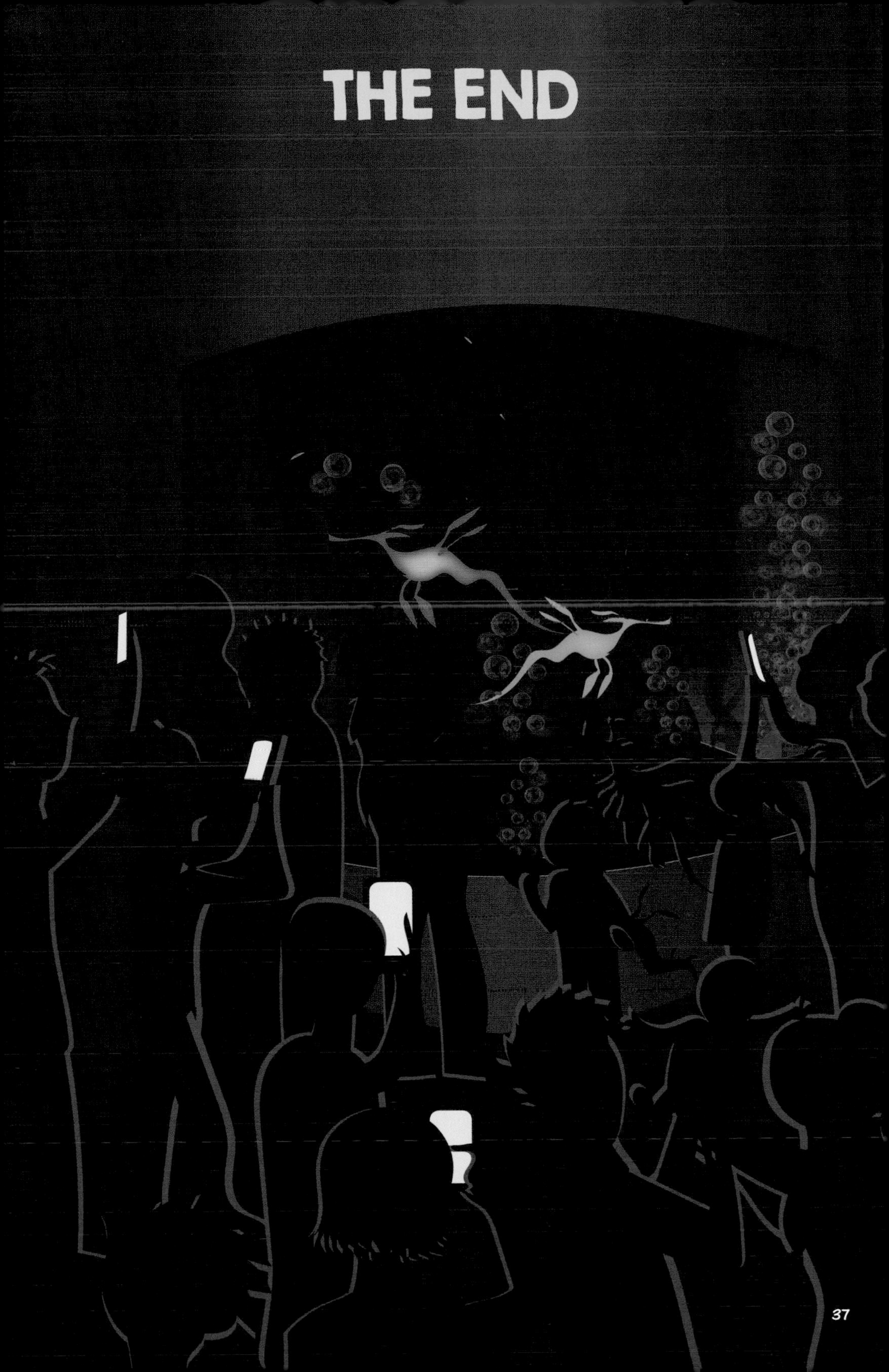
THE END

ANATOMY OF THE Coho Salmon

(delicious no matter the method of cooking)

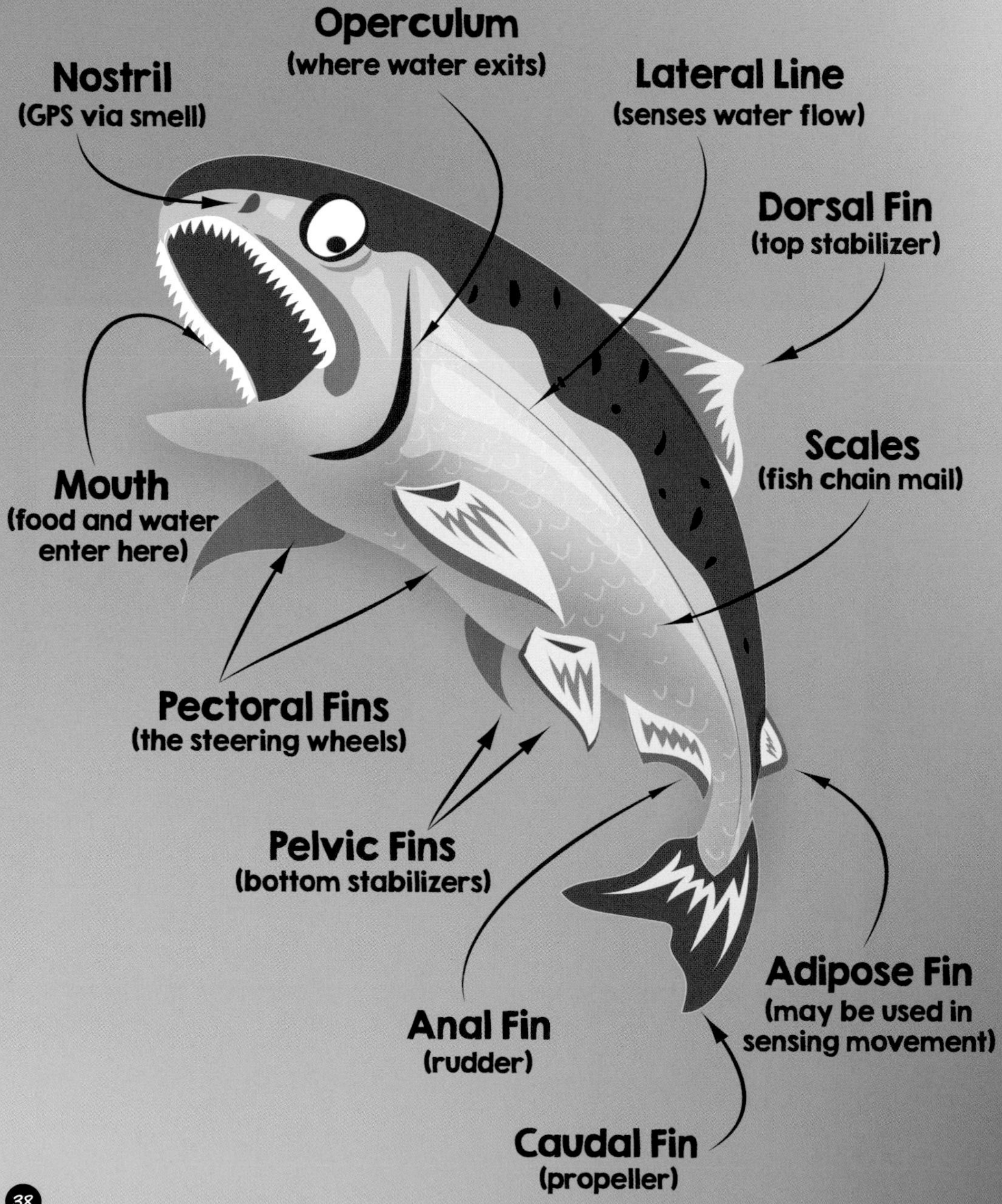
Operculum
(where water exits)
Nostril
(GPS via smell)
Lateral Line
(senses water flow)
Dorsal Fin
(top stabilizer)
Scales
(fish chain mail)
Mouth
(food and water enter here)
Pectoral Fins
(the steering wheels)
Pelvic Fins
(bottom stabilizers)
Adipose Fin
(may be used in sensing movement)
Anal Fin
(rudder)
Caudal Fin
(propeller)

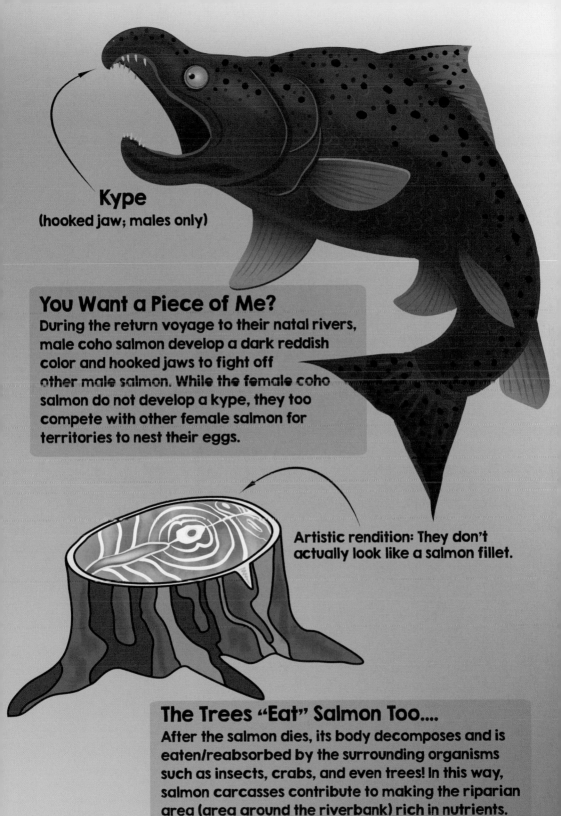

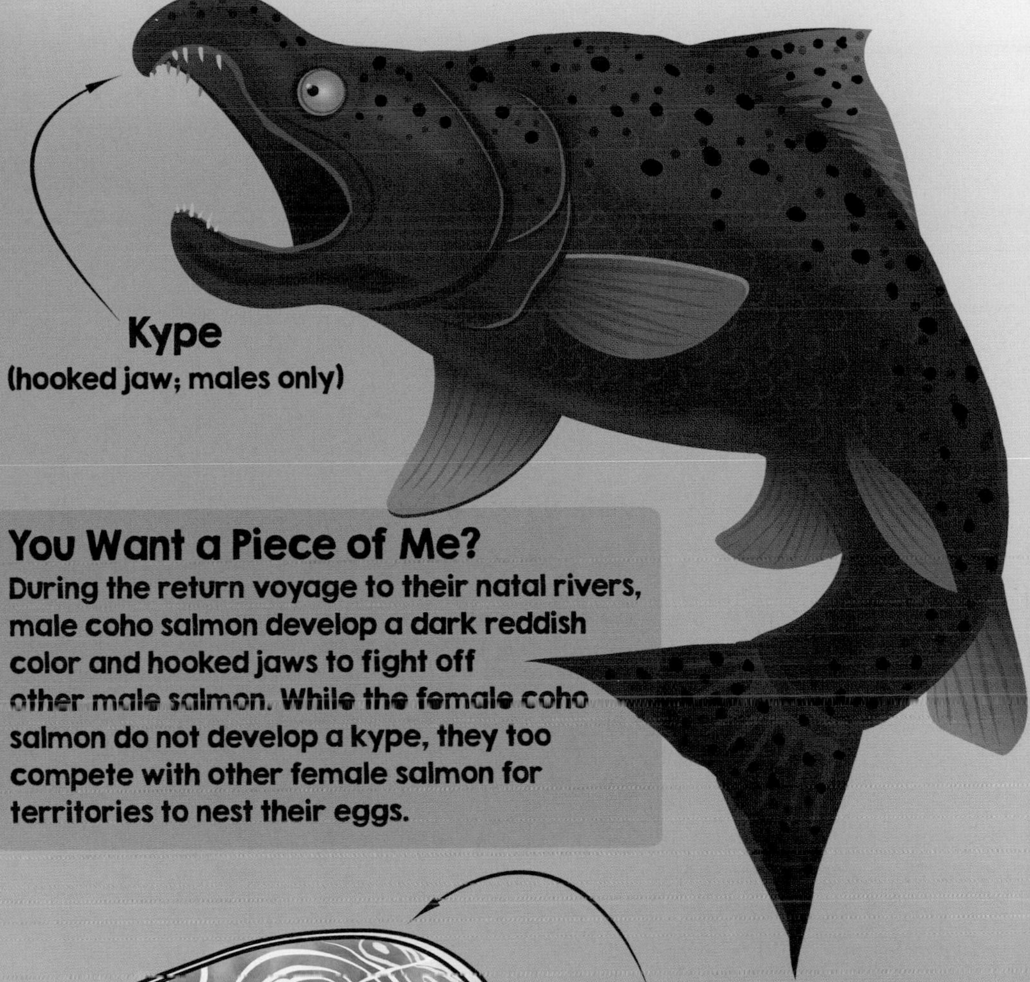
Kype
(hooked jaw; males only)

You Want a Piece of Me?

During the return voyage to their natal rivers, male coho salmon develop a dark reddish color and hooked jaws to fight off other male salmon. While the female coho salmon do not develop a kype, they too compete with other female salmon for territories to nest their eggs.

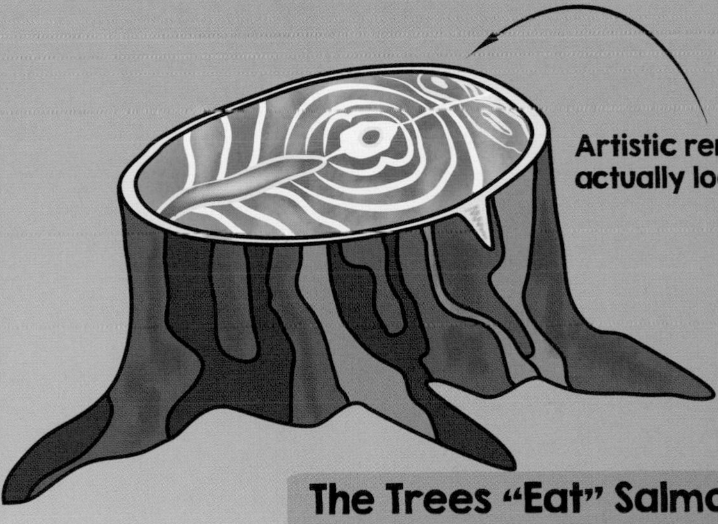

Artistic rendition: They don't actually look like a salmon fillet.

The Trees "Eat" Salmon Too....

After the salmon dies, its body decomposes and is eaten/reabsorbed by the surrounding organisms such as insects, crabs, and even trees! In this way, salmon carcasses contribute to making the riparian area (area around the riverbank) rich in nutrients.

The Life Cycle of the
Sockeye Salmon

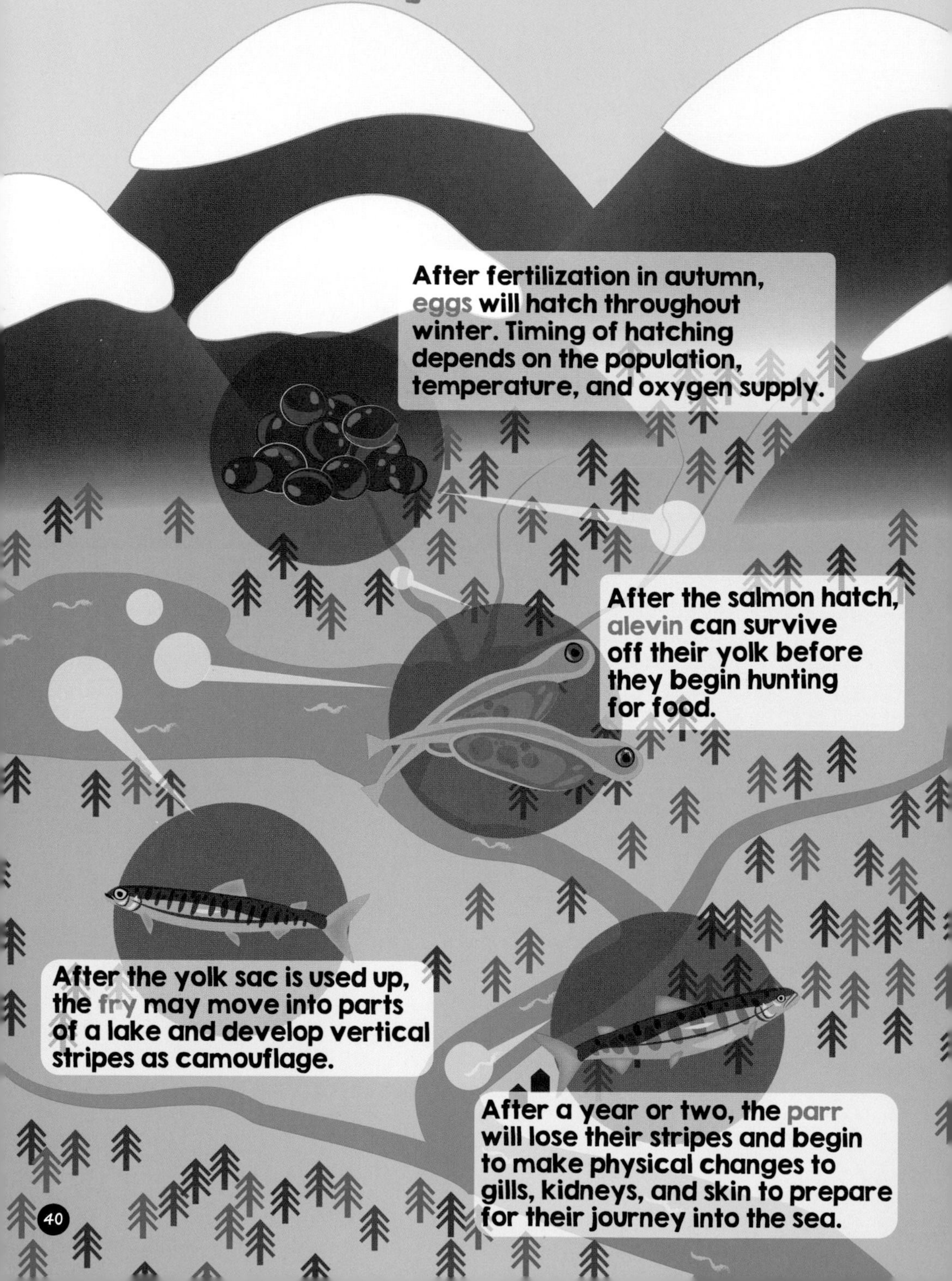

After fertilization in autumn, eggs will hatch throughout winter. Timing of hatching depends on the population, temperature, and oxygen supply.

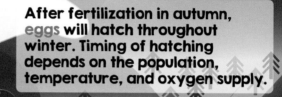

After the salmon hatch, alevin can survive off their yolk before they begin hunting for food.

After the yolk sac is used up, the fry may move into parts of a lake and develop vertical stripes as camouflage.

After a year or two, the parr will lose their stripes and begin to make physical changes to gills, kidneys, and skin to prepare for their journey into the sea.

As salmon move downstream through a dam, they are often injured by the turbines, grates, and even the fall. The pressure of the water being compressed as it goes by can cause barotrauma (injuries caused by rapid changes in pressure).

Adapted for the saline ocean, smolt begin to move downstream throughout spring.

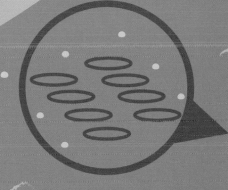

Sockeye salmon are not readily farmed, but coho, Chinook, and Atlantic salmon are kept in net pens off the coast. Salmon farming benefits the local economy, but it also spreads parasites to wild smolt and adult salmon, causing stress and increased mortality.

Adult salmon will spend between one and four years in the ocean feeding on tiny animals such as krill. Where they go exactly is still a bit of a mystery.

Though the salmon benefits from the plentiful food in the ocean, there are also many predators such as the salmon shark.

The salmon sold at markets are caught from the ocean before they start their spawning transformation. As they begin changing and turning red, their flesh quality (and therefore value) decreases.

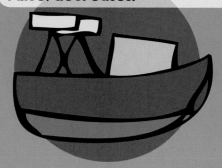

After growing in the ocean, spawning adults will journey back to their natal streams in autumn. Salmon turn red as they move their energy from muscles to their skin and gonads (sperm and eggs). Males even develop a hump and a hooked jaw to be more successful at mating.

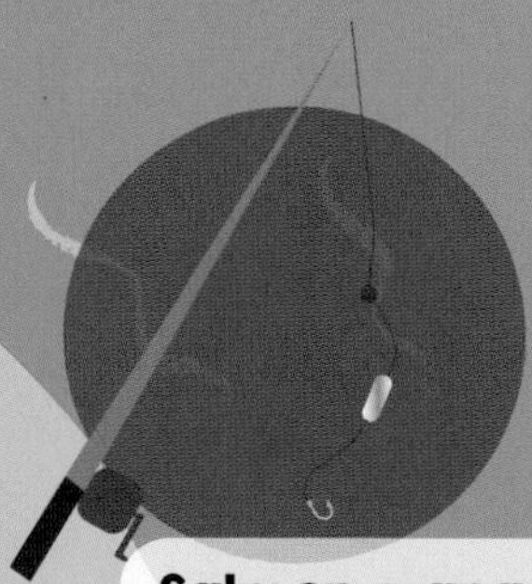

Salmon managers use information such as river temperature and the number of returning sockeye salmon to determine whether to open the season to recreational fishing.

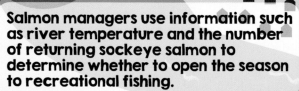

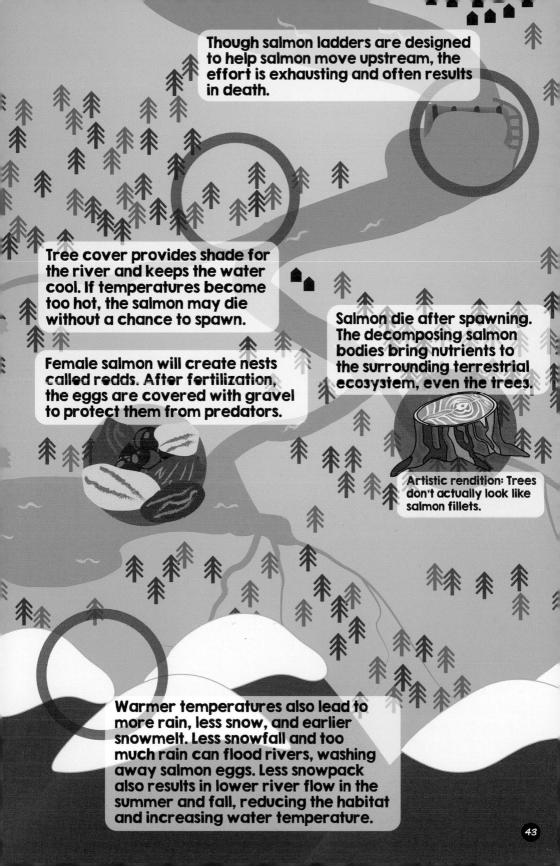

Though salmon ladders are designed to help salmon move upstream, the effort is exhausting and often results in death.

Tree cover provides shade for the river and keeps the water cool. If temperatures become too hot, the salmon may die without a chance to spawn.

Salmon die after spawning. The decomposing salmon bodies bring nutrients to the surrounding terrestrial ecosystem, even the trees.

Female salmon will create nests called redds. After fertilization, the eggs are covered with gravel to protect them from predators.

Artistic rendition: Trees don't actually look like salmon fillets.

Warmer temperatures also lead to more rain, less snow, and earlier snowmelt. Less snowfall and too much rain can flood rivers, washing away salmon eggs. Less snowpack also results in lower river flow in the summer and fall, reducing the habitat and increasing water temperature.

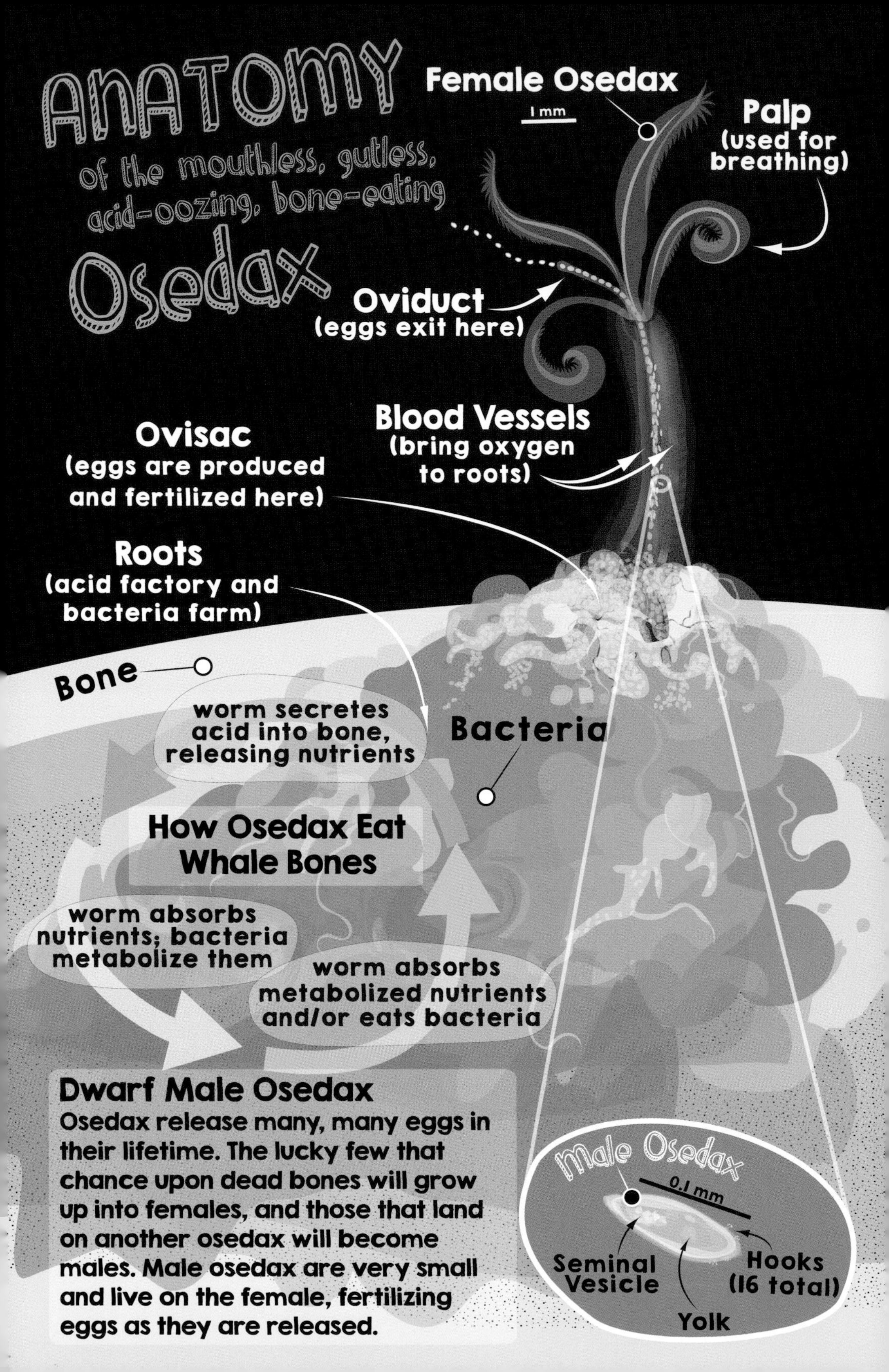
ANATOMY
of the mouthless, gutless, acid-oozing, bone-eating
Osedax
Female Osedax
1 mm
Palp (used for breathing)
Oviduct (eggs exit here)
Blood Vessels (bring oxygen to roots)
Ovisac (eggs are produced and fertilized here)
Roots (acid factory and bacteria farm)
Bone
Bacteria
worm secretes acid into bone, releasing nutrients
How Osedax Eat Whale Bones
worm absorbs nutrients; bacteria metabolize them
worm absorbs metabolized nutrients and/or eats bacteria
Male Osedax
0.1 mm
Seminal Vesicle
Yolk
Hooks (16 total)

Dwarf Male Osedax

Osedax release many, many eggs in their lifetime. The lucky few that chance upon dead bones will grow up into females, and those that land on another osedax will become males. Male osedax are very small and live on the female, fertilizing eggs as they are released.

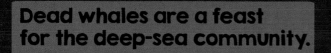

Dead whales are a feast for the deep-sea community.

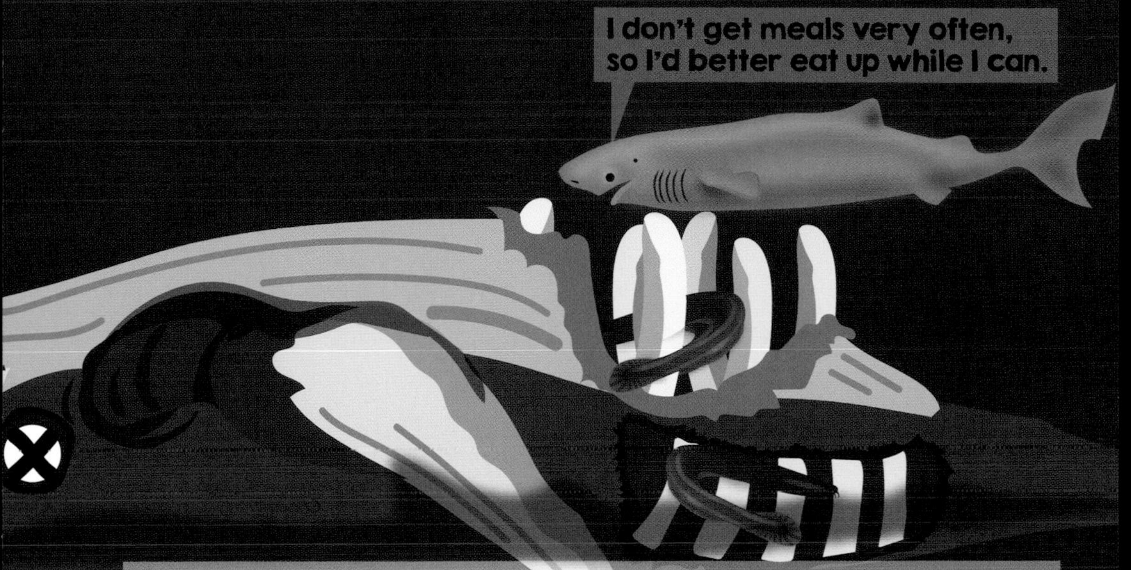
I don't get meals very often, so I'd better eat up while I can.

When big animals like whales die, they often sink and land in the deep sea. The meat is eaten by scavengers like hagfish and sleeper sharks.

Some time later...

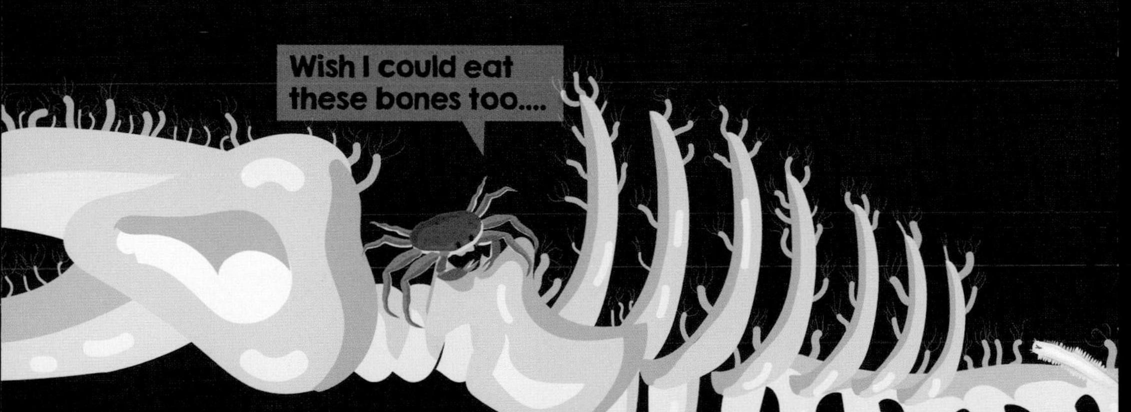
Wish I could eat these bones too....

After the meat is eaten, the decaying bones provide food for bacteria, mussels, crabs, and worms. It is in these decaying patches of whale bones that scientists discovered the osedax. With the help of its symbiotic bacteria, the osedax can dissolve whale bones and absorb their nutrients.

ANATOMY OF THE Market Squid

(tastes great with fried batter and lime)

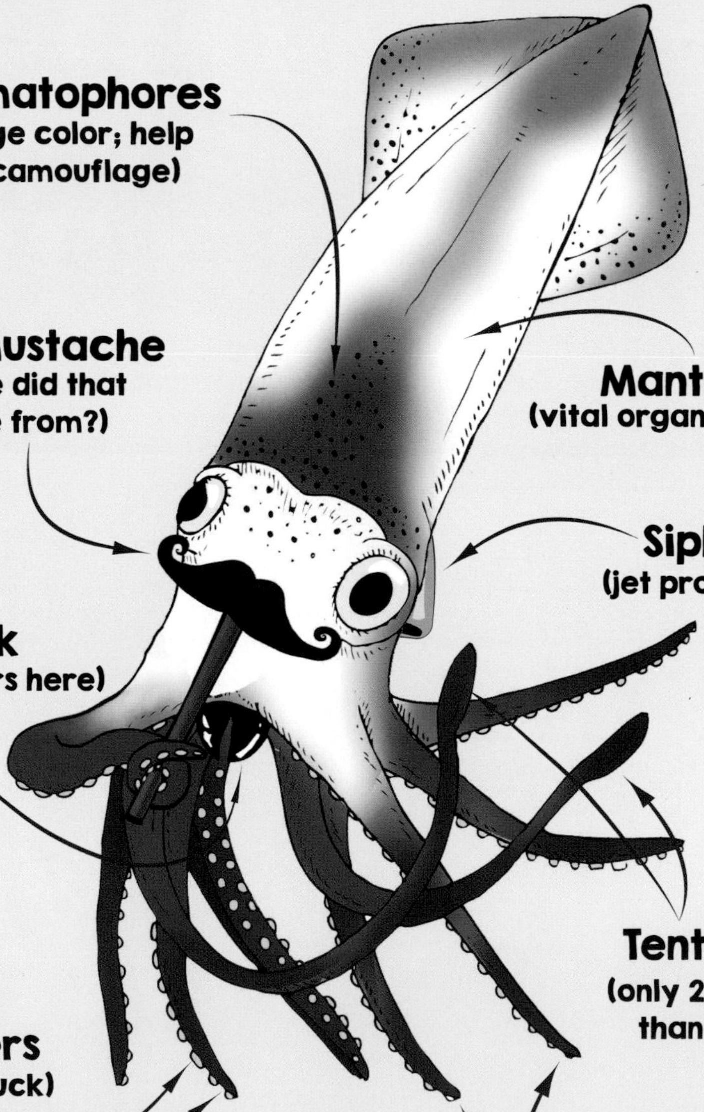
Fin
(guides its movements)
Chromatophores
(change color; help with camouflage)
Fake Mustache
(where did that come from?)
Mantle
(vital organs inside)
Siphon
(jet propeller)
Beak
(food enters here)
Tentacles
(only 2; longer than arms)
Suckers
(these suck)
Arms
(8 in total; shorter than tentacles)

Party on the Shelf

The continental shelf is a relatively flat seafloor generally no deeper than 150 meters. Here, market squid congregate in massive groups to mate and lay their eggs on the sandy bottoms. Sadly, all squid will die shortly after mating or are caught by predators and fishermen (and end up as calamari).

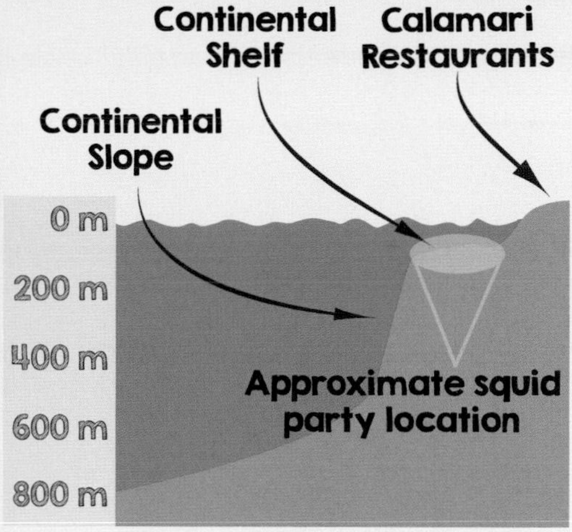
Continental Shelf
Calamari Restaurants
Continental Slope
0 m
200 m
400 m
600 m
800 m
Approximate squid party location

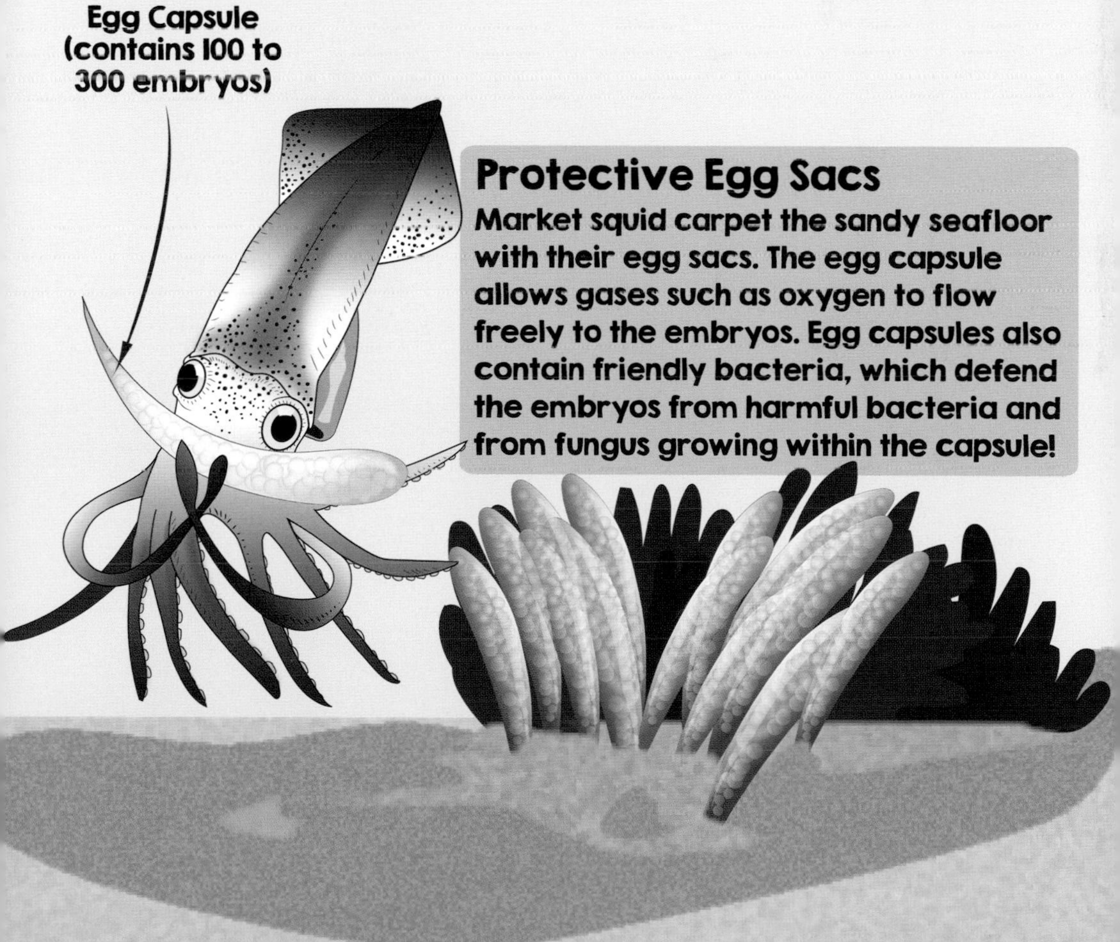
Egg Capsule (contains 100 to 300 embryos)

Protective Egg Sacs

Market squid carpet the sandy seafloor with their egg sacs. The egg capsule allows gases such as oxygen to flow freely to the embryos. Egg capsules also contain friendly bacteria, which defend the embryos from harmful bacteria and from fungus growing within the capsule!

Market Squid Embryos Can Handle Stress, Yo

During mating season, market squid gather in huge numbers to breed.

Squid

Egg Capsules

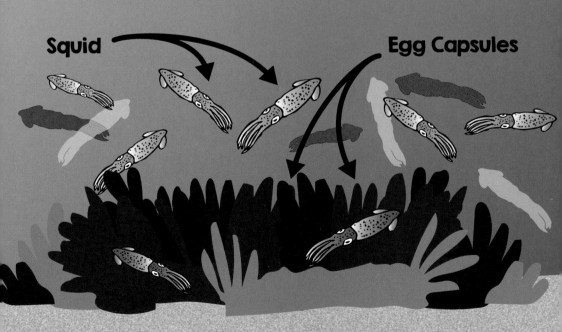

Squid anchor their fertilized egg capsules onto the sandy bottom.

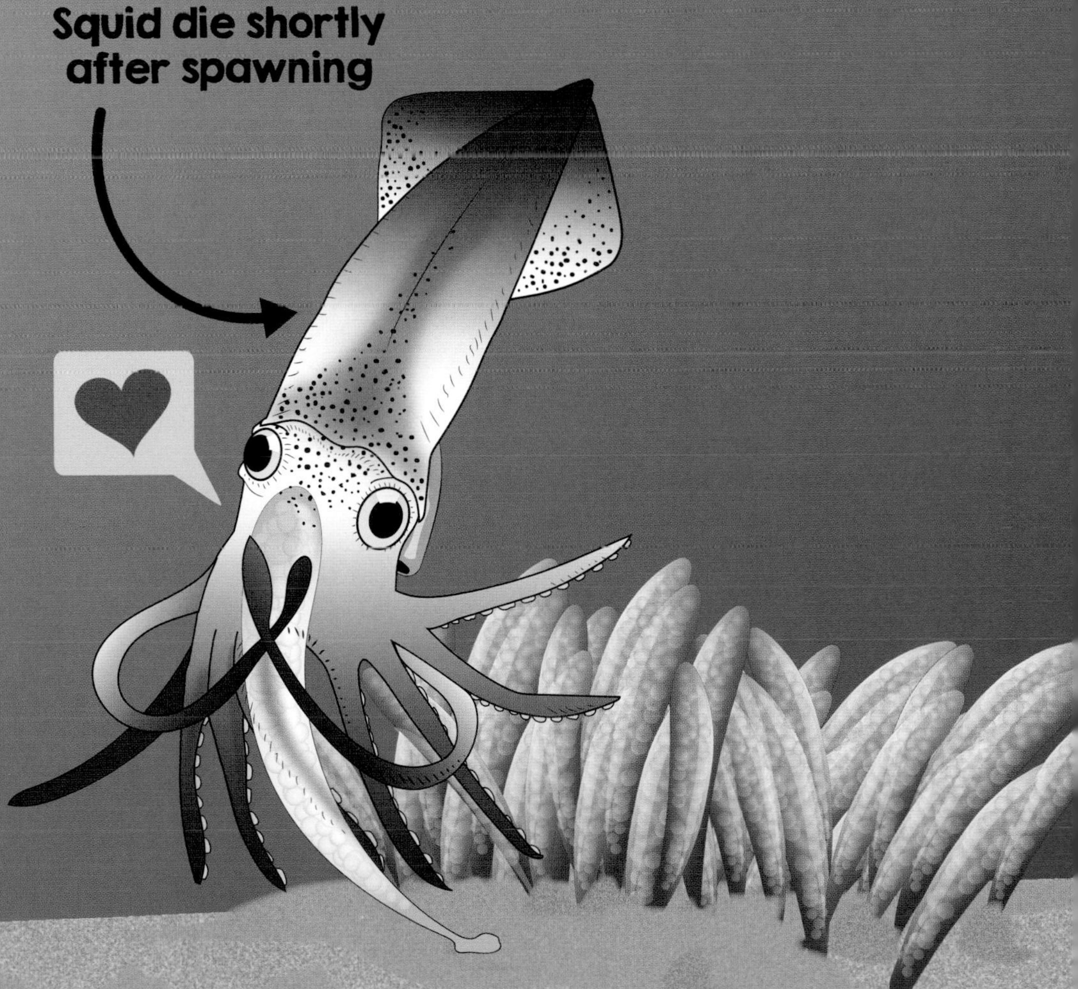
Squid die shortly after spawning

Like many other animals, baby squid need a steady supply of oxygen to thrive.

More specifically, gas exchange is necessary to remove carbon dioxide (CO_2) and restore oxygen (O_2) levels.

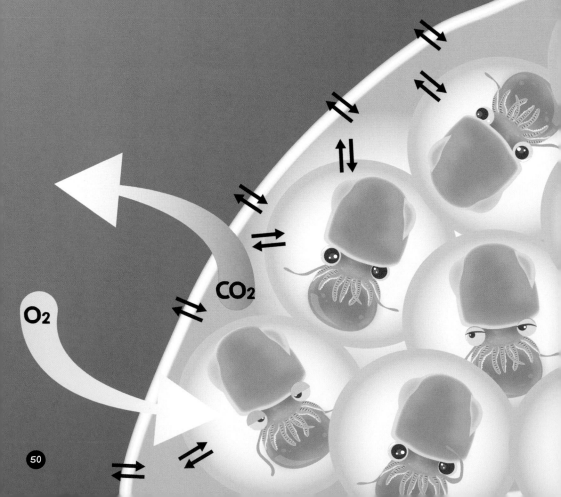

CO_2

O_2

Gas exchange occurs as the ocean current sways the anchored egg capsule.

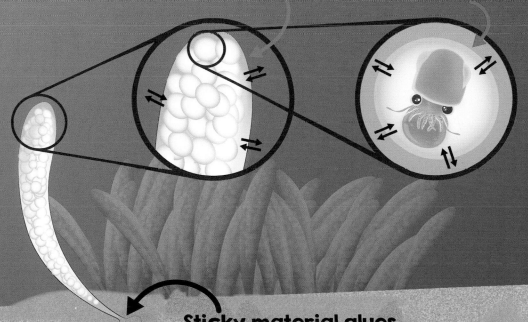

Gas passes through both egg capsule and chorion

Sticky material glues the egg capsule to seafloor

However, ocean mixing sometimes exposes baby squid to oxygen-poor and low-pH (high in CO_2) conditions.

Normal Condition
(normal O_2 and pH level)

O_2: 190 μM; pH: 7.90
O_2: 70 μM; pH: 7.65

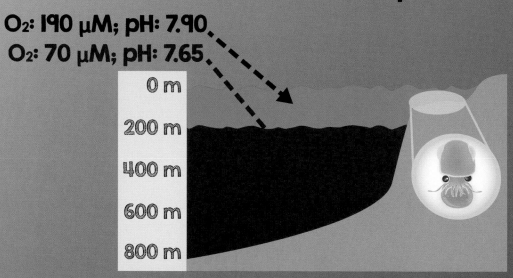

0 m
200 m
400 m
600 m
800 m

Upwelling Condition
(low O_2 and pH level)

O_2: 190 μM; pH: 7.90
O_2: 70 μM; pH: 7.65

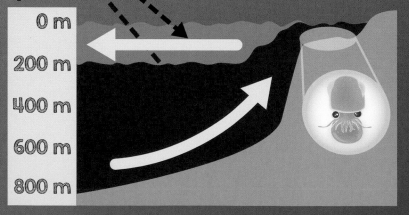

0 m
200 m
400 m
600 m
800 m

How do squid embryos respond to combined low O$_2$ and low pH?

Even though squid embryos develop more slowly when exposed to both low O$_2$ and low pH, both groups eventually grow to similar sizes.

Normal Condition
O$_2$: 242 µM; pH: 7.93

Low O$_2$ and Low pH
O$_2$: 80 µM; pH: 7.57

* Longer mantle length and shorter head width are characteristics of a more developed squid embryo.

How do low O_2 and pH independently affect squid embryos?

Even though both groups were similar in size, low pH embryos use more yolk than low O_2 embryos.

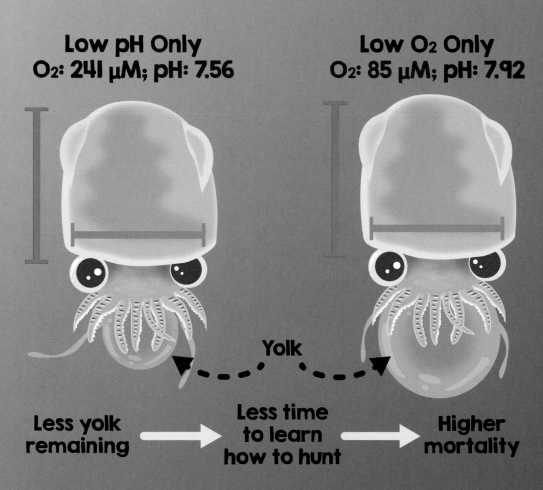

Low pH Only
O_2: 241 μM; pH: 7.56

Low O_2 Only
O_2: 85 μM; pH: 7.92

Yolk

Less yolk remaining → Less time to learn how to hunt → Higher mortality

HOWEVER, this scenario rarely occurs in the wild.

Scientists found squid embryos develop better under combined low O_2 and low pH stress compared with an individual stressor (only low pH or only low O_2).

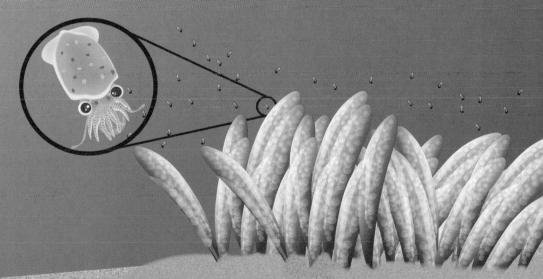

Since low O_2 and low pH almost always occur together in their habitat, the results suggest market squid are highly adapted to their local ecosystem.

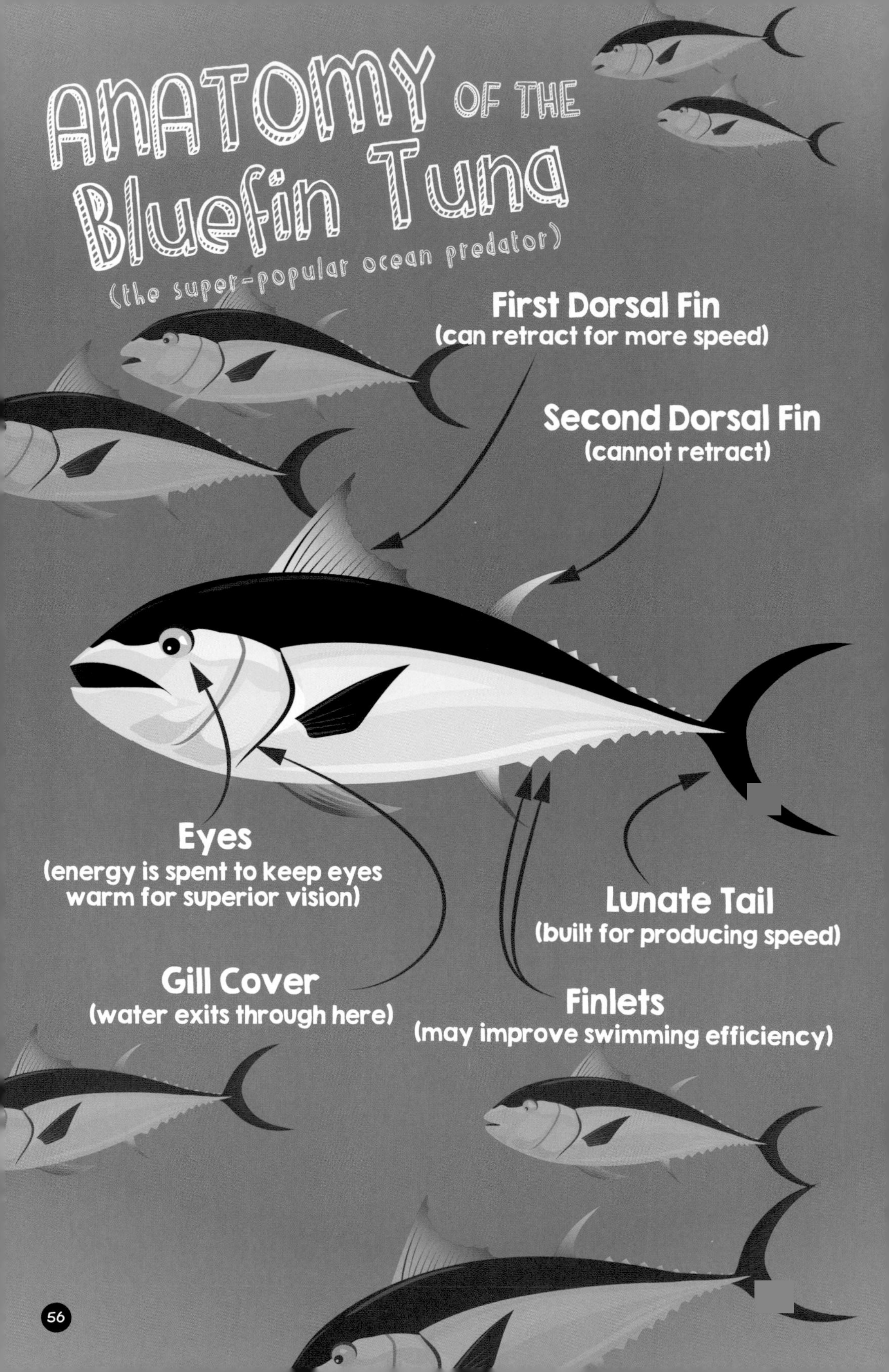
Anatomy of the Bluefin Tuna
(the super-popular ocean predator)
First Dorsal Fin
(can retract for more speed)
Second Dorsal Fin
(cannot retract)
Eyes
(energy is spent to keep eyes warm for superior vision)
Lunate Tail
(built for producing speed)
Gill Cover
(water exits through here)
Finlets
(may improve swimming efficiency)

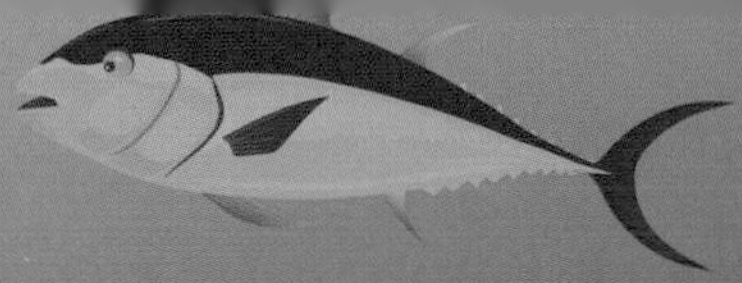

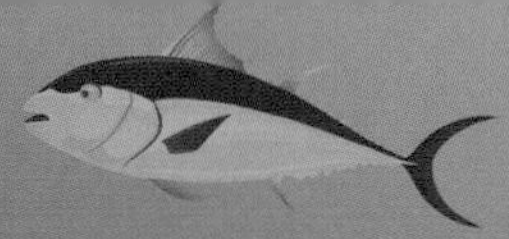

Partly Warm-Blooded

Compared with the surrounding water, bluefin tuna have a warmer body temperature. This allows tuna to see, react, and swim faster than cold-blooded fish. But they are classified as regional endotherms, meaning they heat only certain regions in their body (like the eyes, brain, and core muscles).

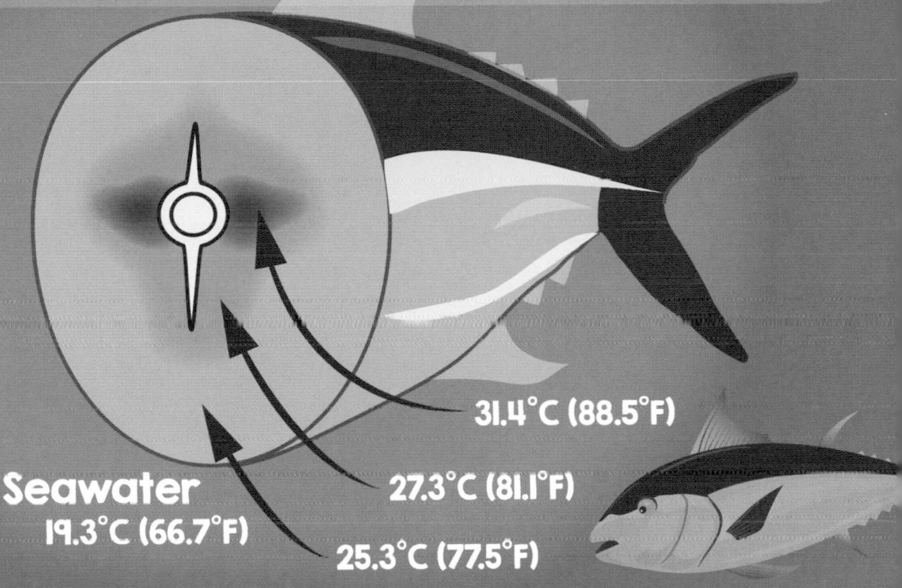
31.4°C (88.5°F)
Seawater
19.3°C (66.7°F)
27.3°C (81.1°F)
25.3°C (77.5°F)

Pollutant Accumulation

Pollutants are found all over the ocean. Oftentimes, they are locked in animals and cannot be naturally broken down. As big fish eat smaller fish, pollutants like mercury and lead accumulate—potentially to dangerous levels. Therefore, it is safer for humans to eat smaller fish like sardines and avoid eating too many big predators like tuna.

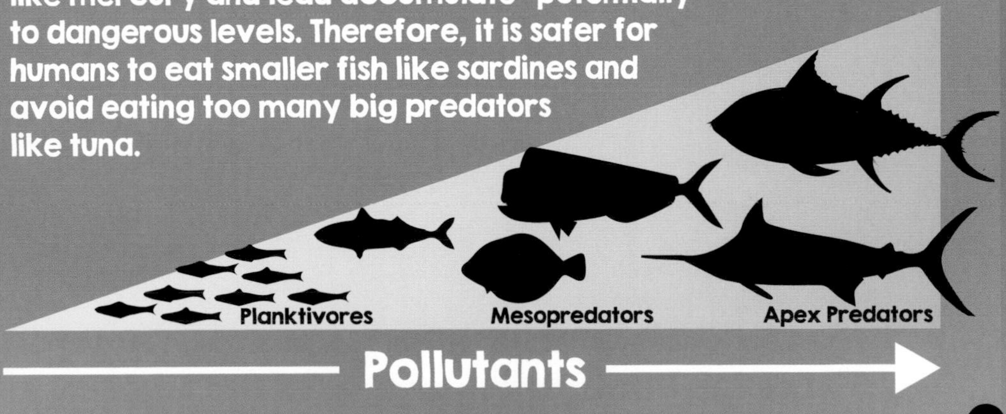
Planktivores
Mesopredators
Apex Predators
Pollutants

ANATOMY OF THE California Grunion

(also found in Baja California)

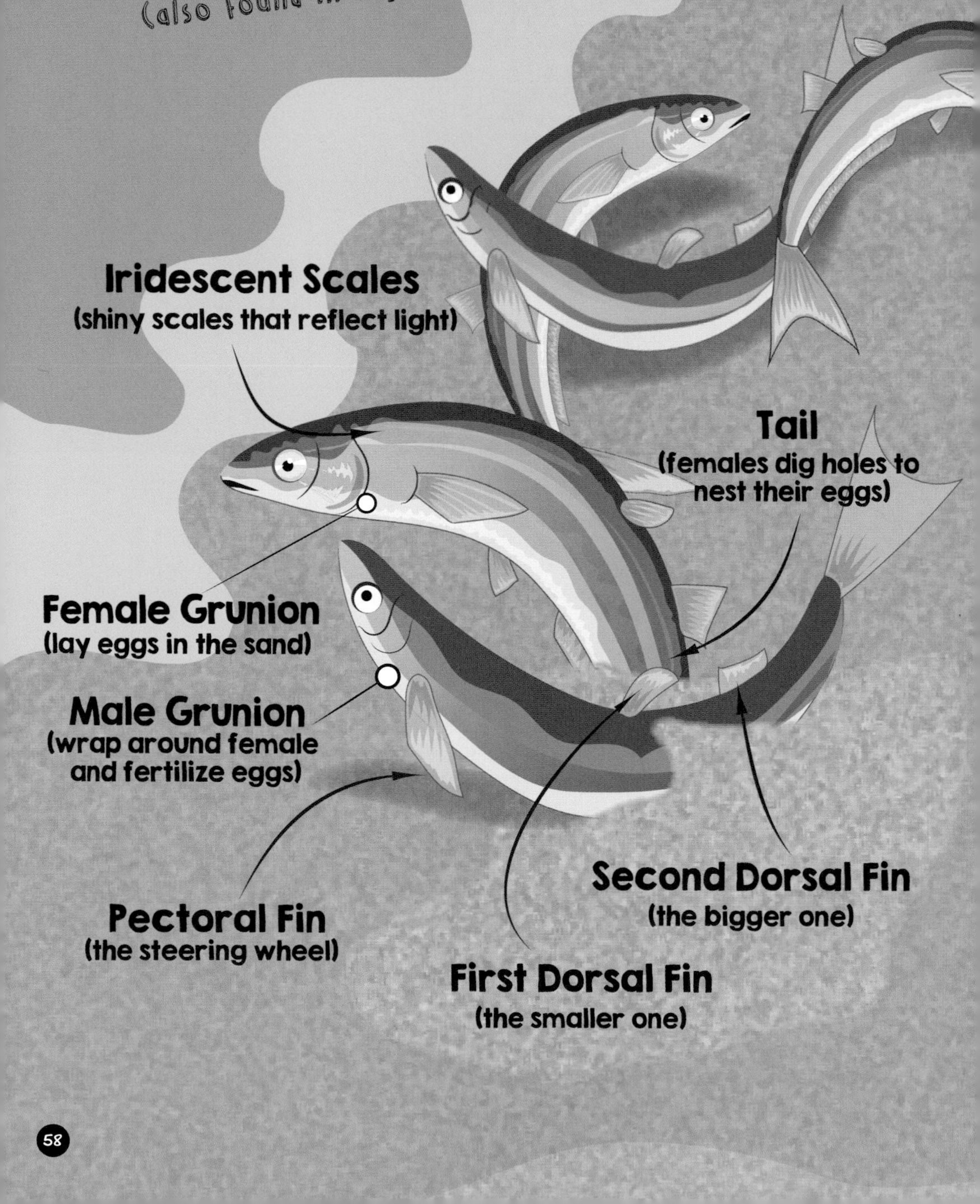

Iridescent Scales
(shiny scales that reflect light)
Tail
(females dig holes to nest their eggs)
Female Grunion
(lay eggs in the sand)
Male Grunion
(wrap around female and fertilize eggs)
Second Dorsal Fin
(the bigger one)
Pectoral Fin
(the steering wheel)
First Dorsal Fin
(the smaller one)

Spawned on Land

During the spring and summer months (March to August), California grunion mate when spring tides occur under the cover of night. When Earth, moon, and sun align, their combined gravitational forces cause the tides to be at their peak, or spring tide. This ensures the grunion eggs will have a safe place to develop when the tides recede.

Moon and sun are at a right angle, resulting in neap tide.

Moon and sun are aligned, resulting in spring tide.

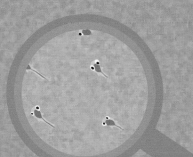

Washed to Sea

It takes about two weeks for the next spring tide to occur. During this time, baby grunion develop in the sand away from water. At the next spring tide, the tides will bring seawater to the eggs. However, seawater isn't enough! The grunion eggs will need to feel the waves crashing above them before they hatch and swim into the ocean.

6 Ways to Check If You Are a Lobster

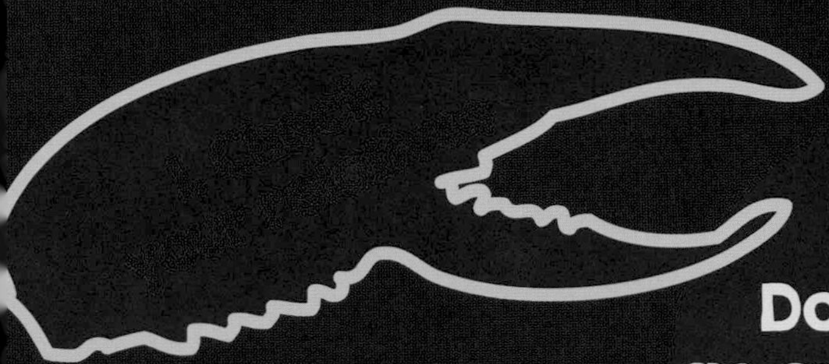

Do you have an extraordinary number of relatives?

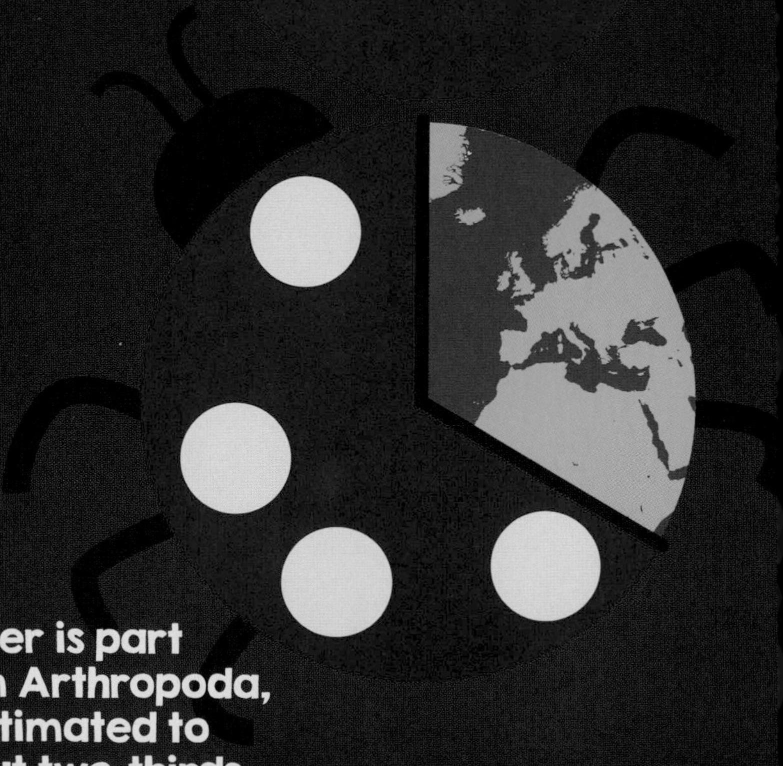

The lobster is part of the phylum Arthropoda, which is estimated to include about two-thirds of the world's animals.

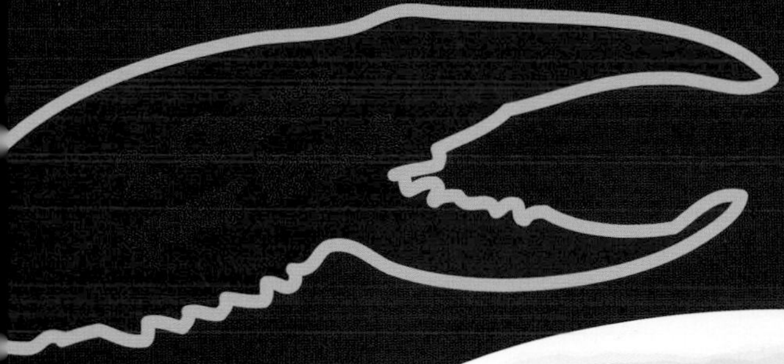

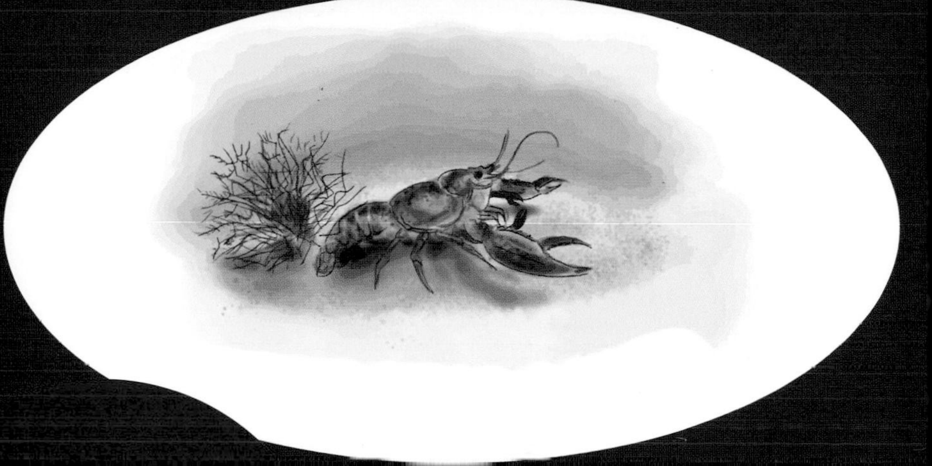

Do you have five pairs of legs? If so, you may be a lobster.

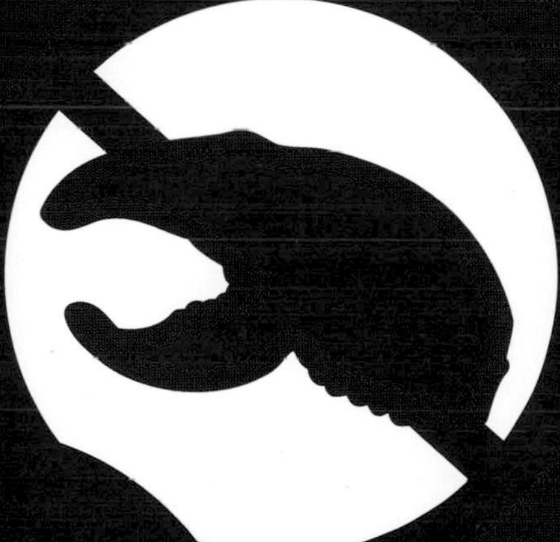

Don't have claws? Some lobsters do not have claws, for example the spiny lobster.

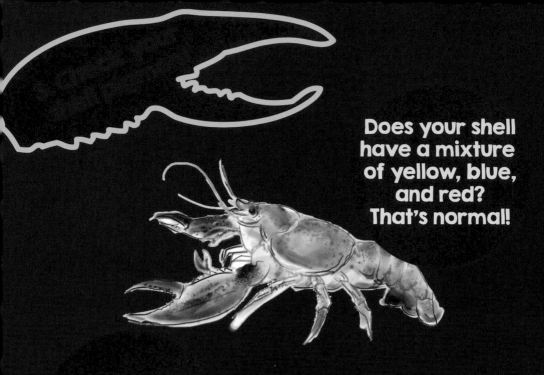

Does your shell have a mixture of yellow, blue, and red? That's normal!

Is your shell covered in blue? Awesome! You're one in 2 million!

Lobsters usually only have red shells after they're cooked. If you are naturally red, you're one in 10 million!

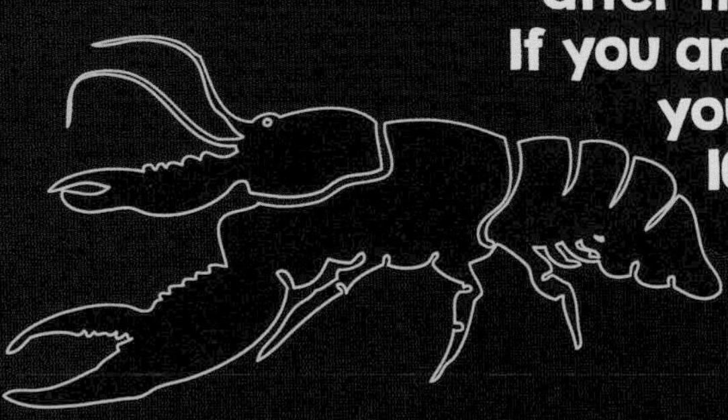

Is your shell coated in yellow? Sweet! You're one in 30 million!

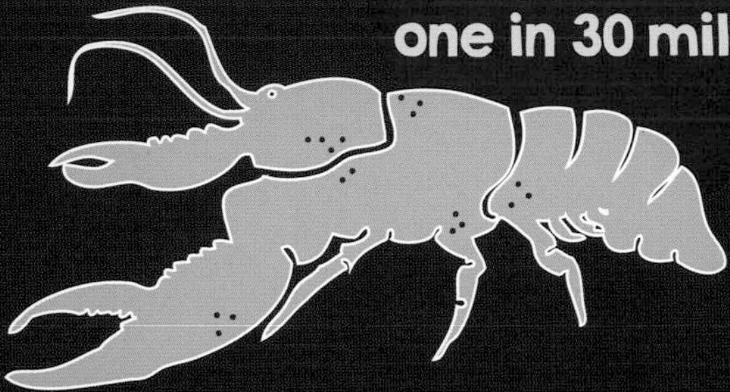

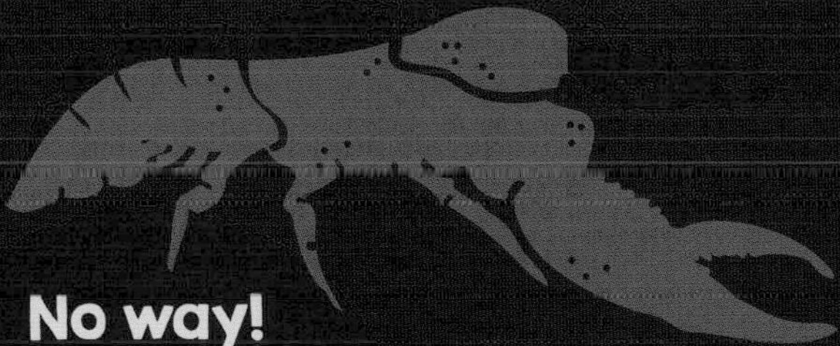

No way! Your shell is two-toned?! That's one in 50 million!

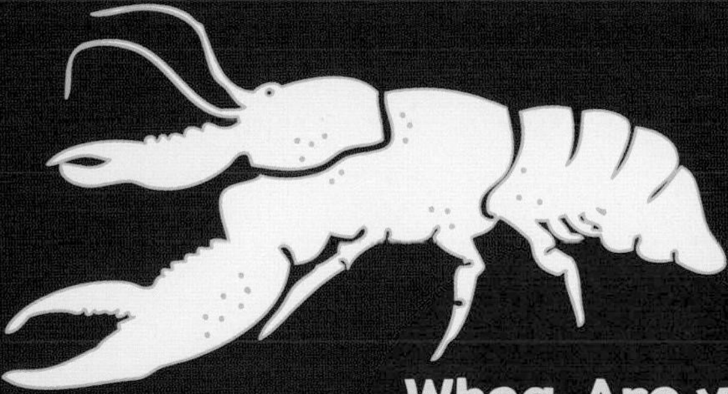

Whoa. Are you all white? Albino lobsters are one in 100 million!

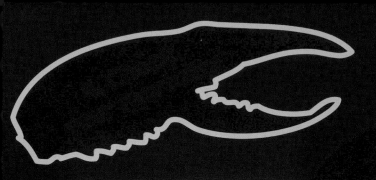

Do you feel as if you aren't aging?

Like turtles, lobsters might have negligible senescence (a very slow rate of aging).

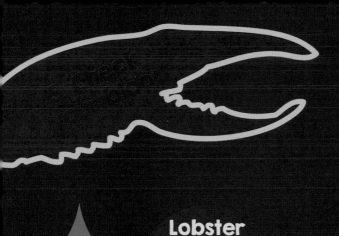

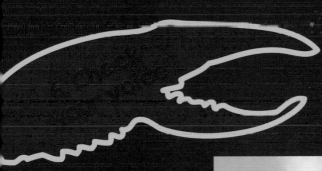

Lobster
blood is
blue because
it contains
copper.

If your
blood turns
red, then you
are not
a lobster.

Lobsters
don't have vocal
cords. Try to
scream and see if
you can hear
yourself.

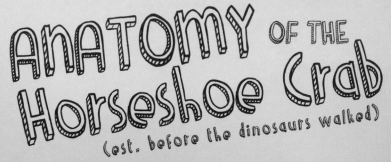

ANATOMY OF THE Horseshoe Crab
(est. before the dinosaurs walked)

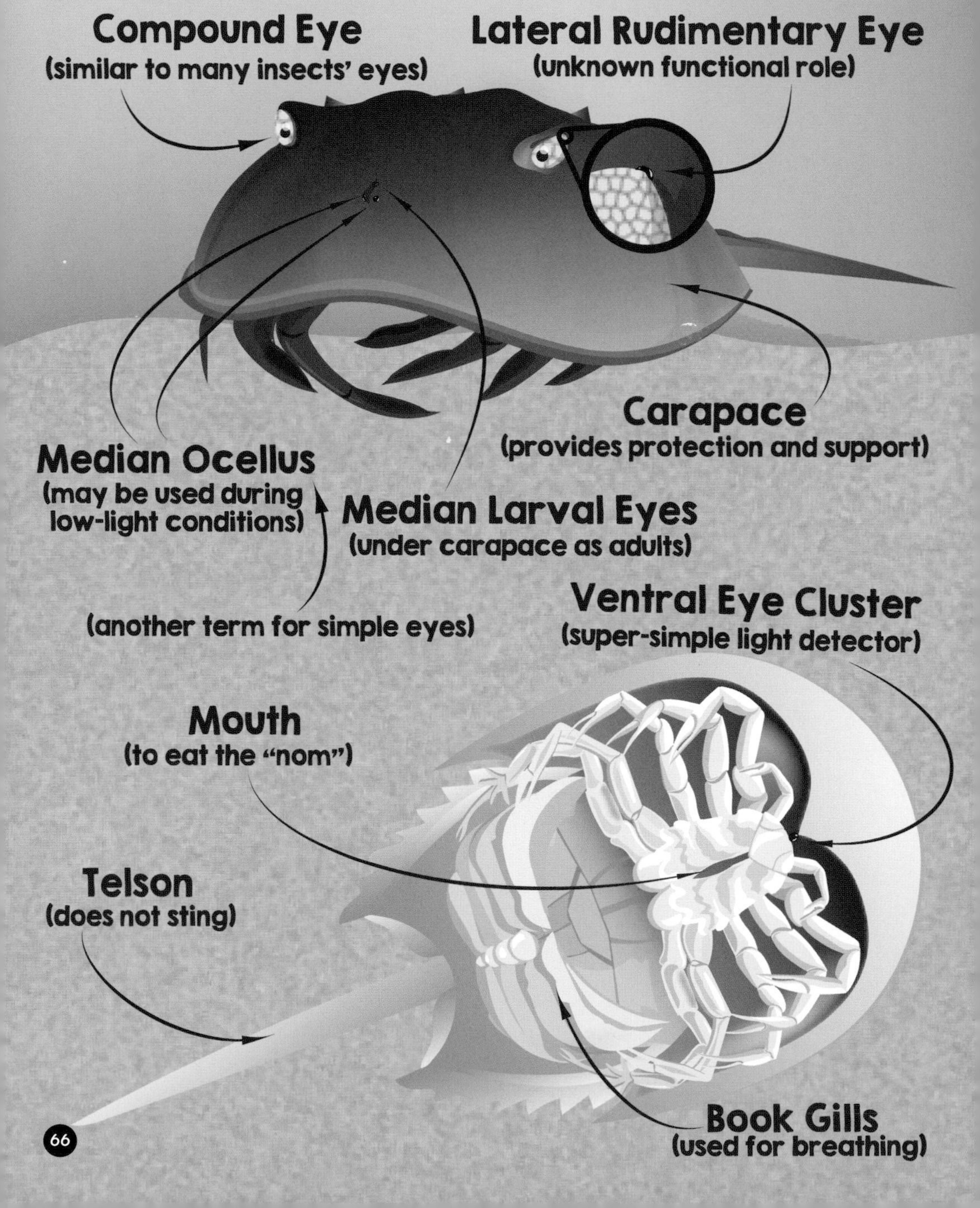

Compound Eye
(similar to many insects' eyes)

Lateral Rudimentary Eye
(unknown functional role)

Carapace
(provides protection and support)

Median Ocellus
(may be used during low-light conditions)

Median Larval Eyes
(under carapace as adults)

(another term for simple eyes)

Ventral Eye Cluster
(super-simple light detector)

Mouth
(to eat the "nom")

Telson
(does not sting)

Book Gills
(used for breathing)

2 eyes
1 clawed pair
of legs

10 eyes
5 clawed pairs
of legs

Not a Crab

Despite their name, horseshoe crabs are more closely related to spiders than to crustaceans. The horseshoe crabs' unique number of eyes and limbs reflect these differences.

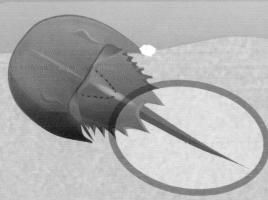

Many Uses of the Telson

✓ Detects surrounding light with photoreceptors

✓ Digging tool

✓ Flips itself right-side up

✗ Receives XM radio signal

Blue Blood Saves Lives

Horseshoe crabs' blue blood will clot when it detects toxin-producing bacteria. Today, it is used to prevent bacterial contamination in surgical tools, pacemakers, and medicine.

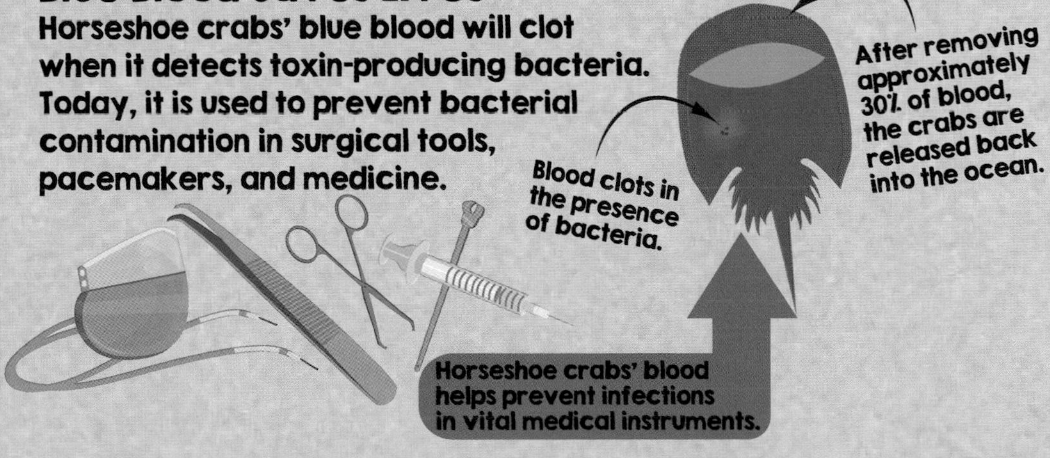

Blood clots in the presence of bacteria.

After removing approximately 30% of blood, the crabs are released back into the ocean.

Horseshoe crabs' blood helps prevent infections in vital medical instruments.

Anatomy of the Yeti Crab

(yes, it likes being this hairy)

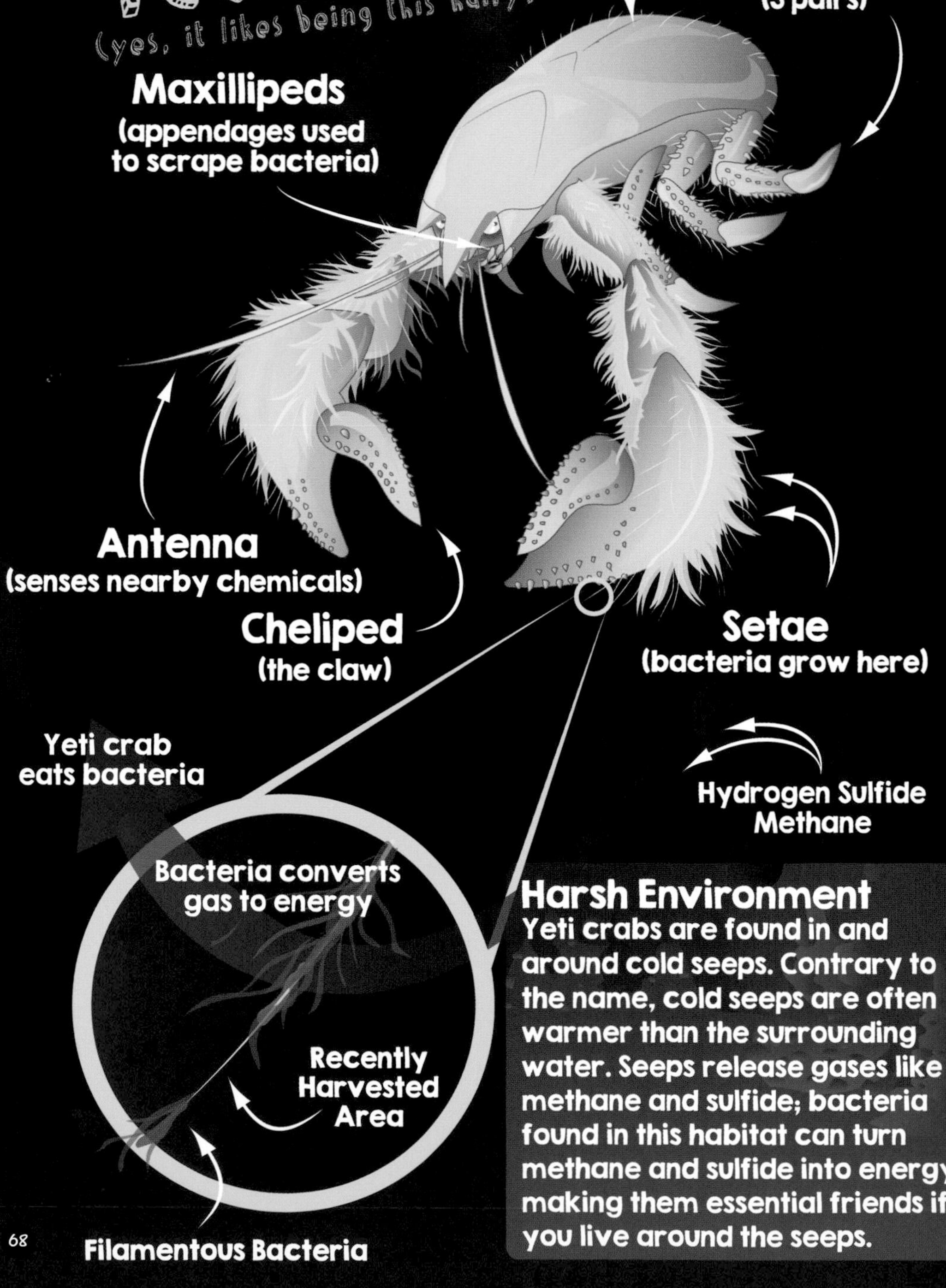

Carapace
(hard outer covering)
Walking Legs
(3 pairs)
Maxillipeds
(appendages used to scrape bacteria)
Antenna
(senses nearby chemicals)
Cheliped
(the claw)
Setae
(bacteria grow here)
Yeti crab eats bacteria
Hydrogen Sulfide
Methane
Bacteria converts gas to energy
Recently Harvested Area
Filamentous Bacteria

Harsh Environment

Yeti crabs are found in and around cold seeps. Contrary to the name, cold seeps are often warmer than the surrounding water. Seeps release gases like methane and sulfide; bacteria found in this habitat can turn methane and sulfide into energy, making them essential friends if you live around the seeps.

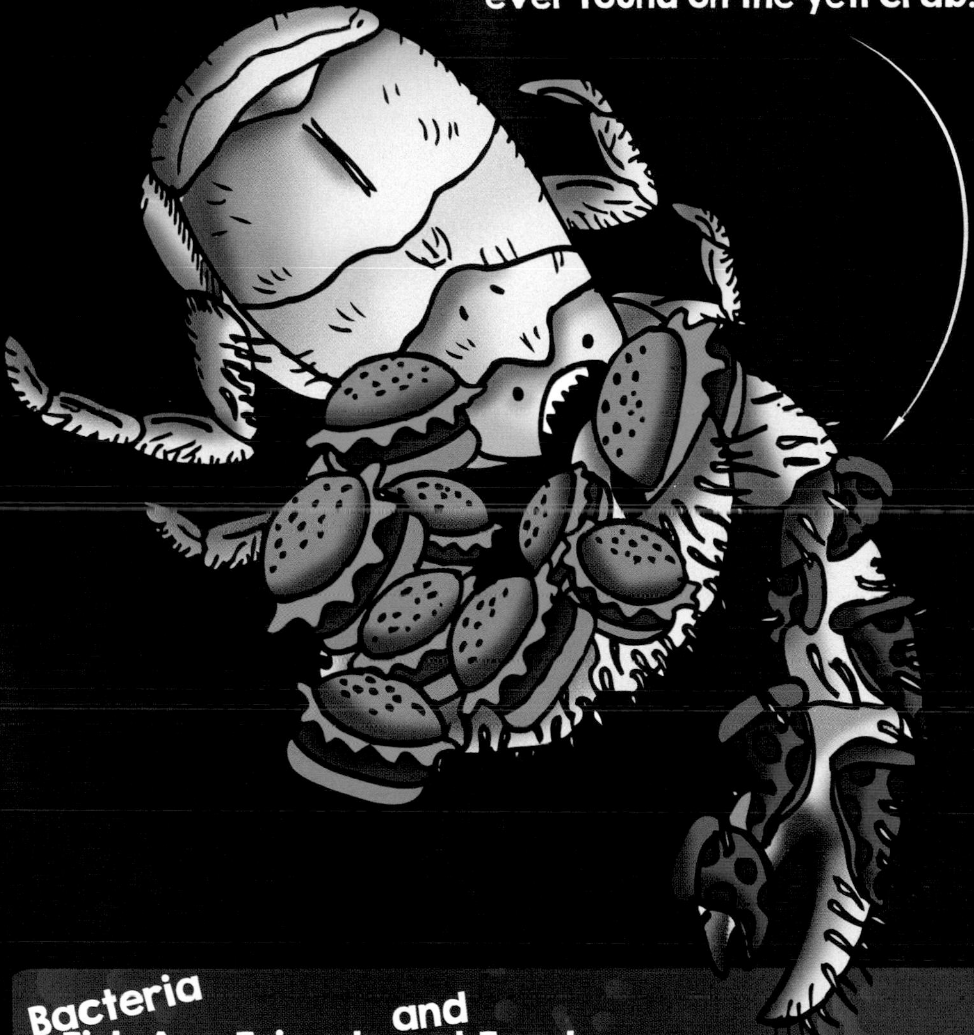
Artistic rendition:
No pizzas or burgers were ever found on the yeti crab....

Bacteria ~~Fish~~ Are Friends, and ~~not~~ Food

To help the bacteria grow, the crab will dance and wave its chelipeds. The crab will eventually harvest the bacteria with its maxillipeds. Alternatively, the bacteria may help the yeti crab detoxify its surrounding water.

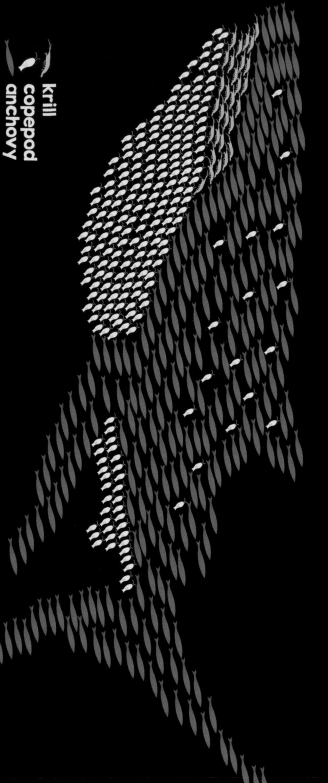

You Are What You Eat
Whale Shark
(Rhincodon typus)

krill
copepod
anchovy

You Are What You Eat

Great White Shark

(Carcharodon carcharias)

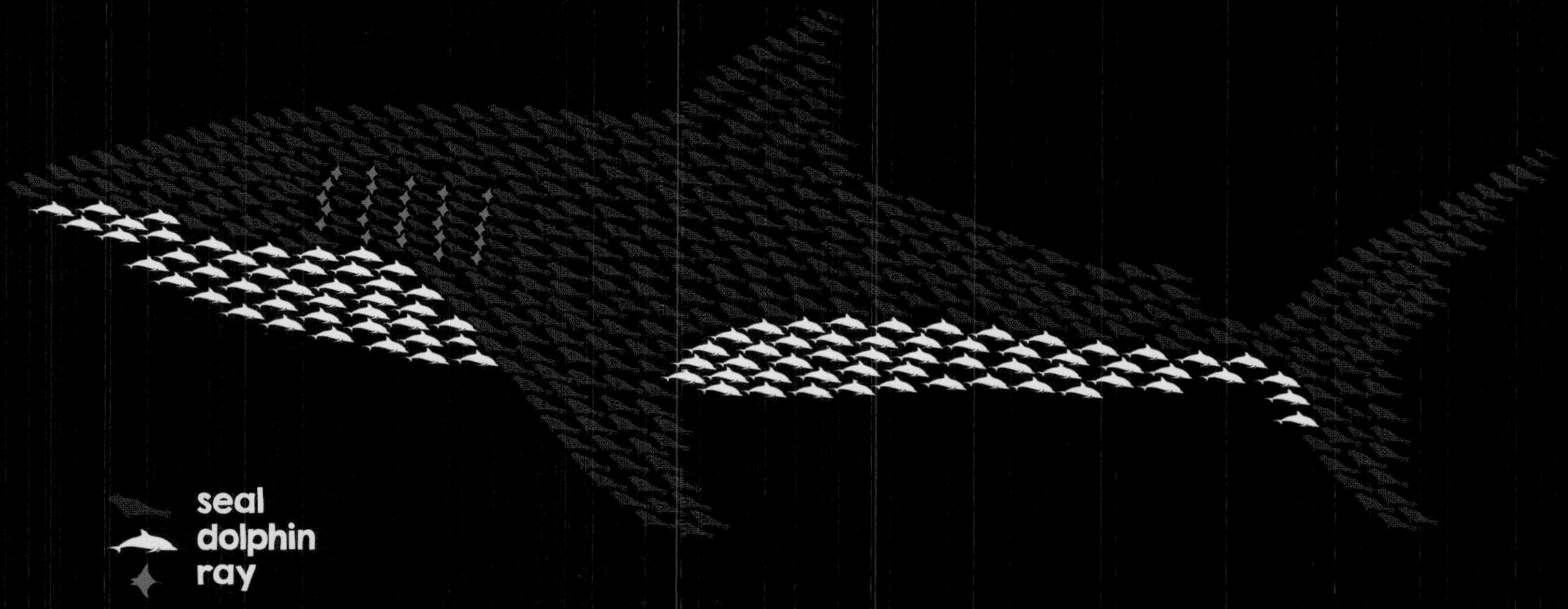
seal
dolphin
ray

Anatomy of the Tuna Crab

(because it's the tuna's favorite snack)

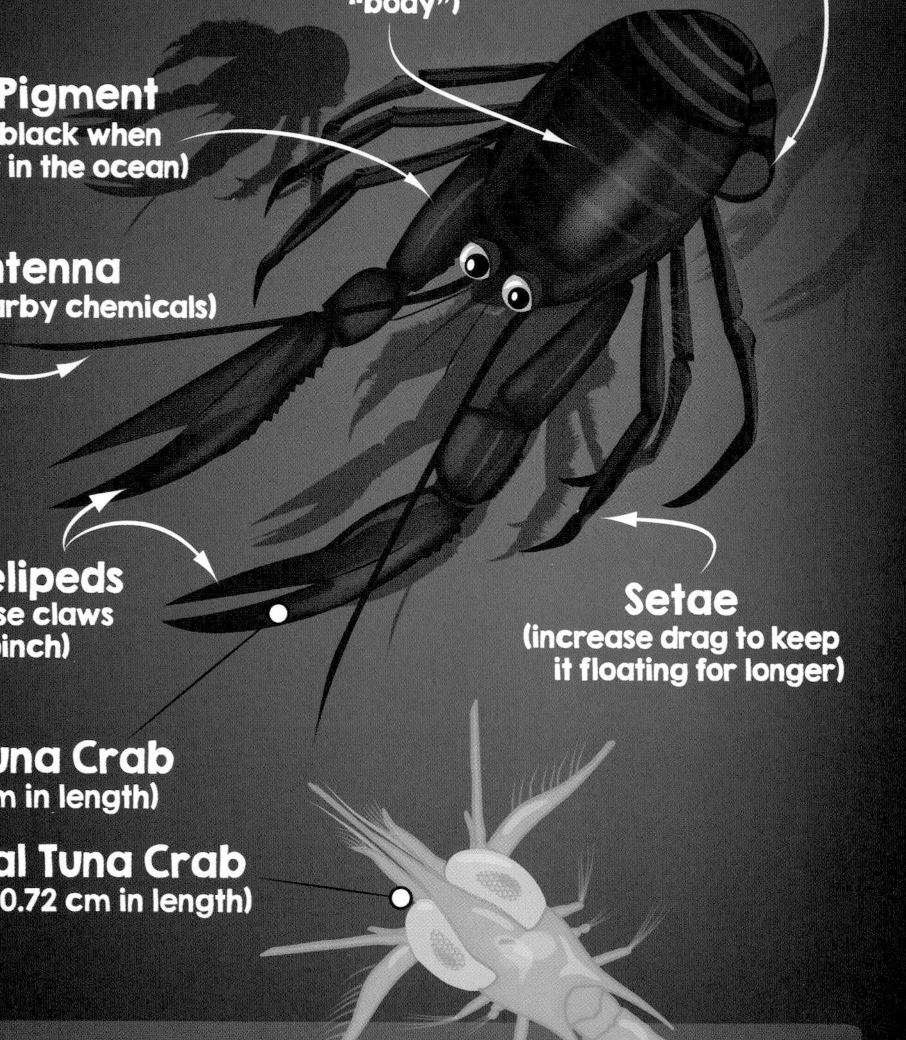
Tail Fan
(they swim backward)
Cephalothorax
(fancy way of saying "body")
Red Pigment
(looks black when deeper in the ocean)
Antenna
(senses nearby chemicals)
Chelipeds
(these claws pinch)
Setae
(increase drag to keep it floating for longer)
Adult Tuna Crab
(2.5 to 13 cm in length)
Larval Tuna Crab
(0.26 to 0.72 cm in length)

Hide Your Kids

Almost everything in the ocean wants to eat the tuna crab... regardless of its age. By being nearly transparent, the tuna crab has a better chance at surviving its early stages.

Late-Night Snacks

Diving deeper to avoid predators means less food to eat, so many (but not all) tuna crabs will hide in deeper water during the day and swim toward the surface to feed on plankton during the night.

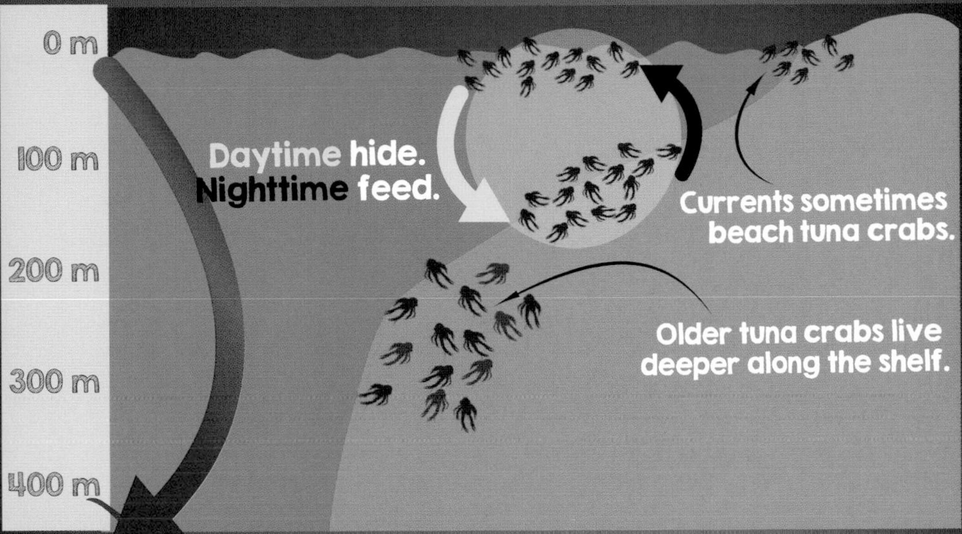

0 m
100 m
200 m
300 m
400 m
Daytime hide.
Nighttime feed.
Currents sometimes beach tuna crabs.
Older tuna crabs live deeper along the shelf.

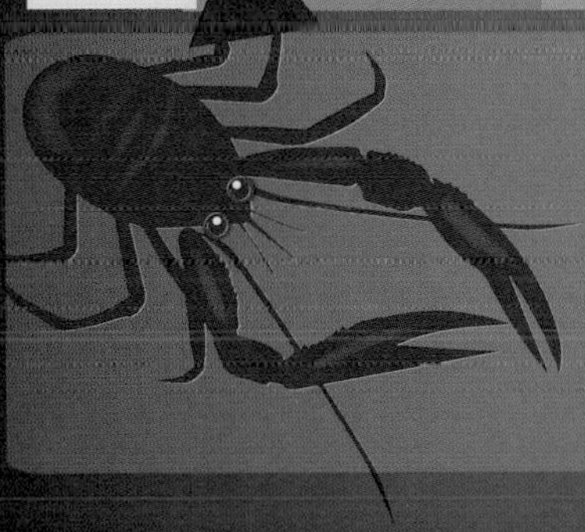

Red Is the New Black

Red light cannot reach very deep into the ocean. While the red tuna crab will stand out in the blue surface ocean, a tuna crab that is deeper in the ocean will appear nearly invisible. This helps the tuna crab avoid becoming a crunchy snack.

Aptly Named

But despite all its adaptations, tuna crabs are often eaten by animals such as tuna (thus the name). One study reports tuna crabs fill up to 85% of the tuna's stomach.

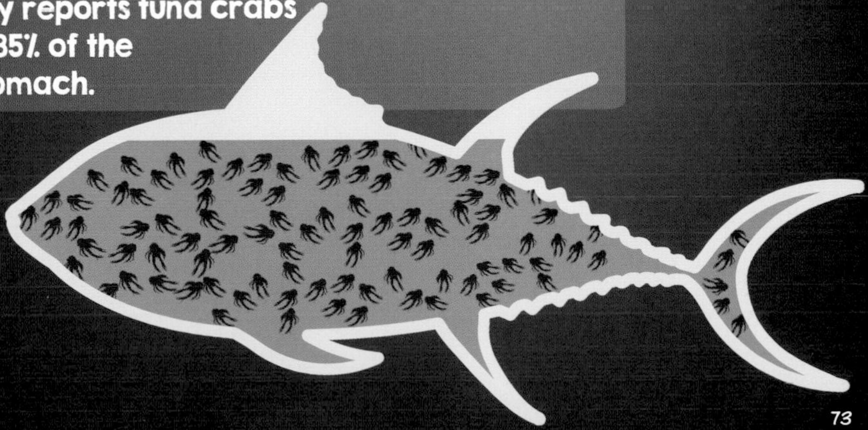

The FALLACY of Sharks

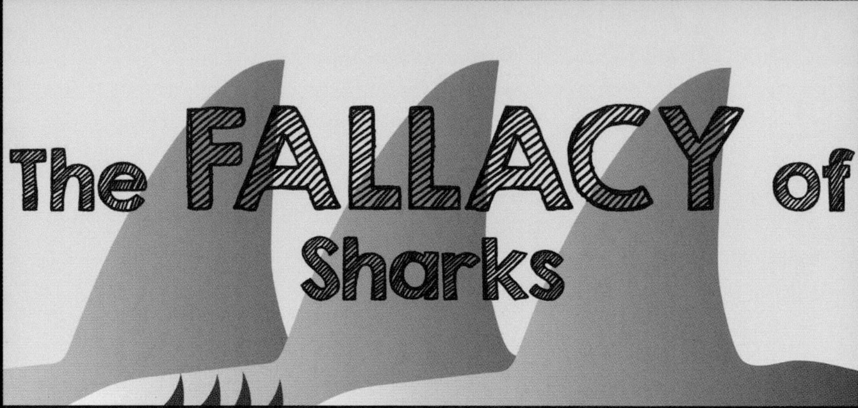

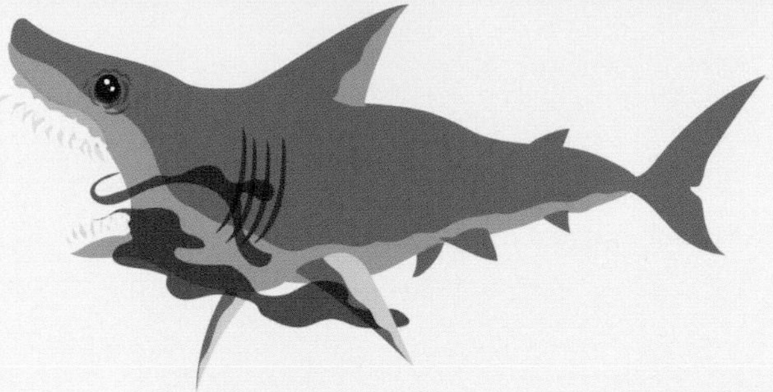

Sharks aren't exactly the friendliest-looking creatures
(which is understandable).

We all know the classic story of sharks: aggressive, bloodthirsty, and destructive.

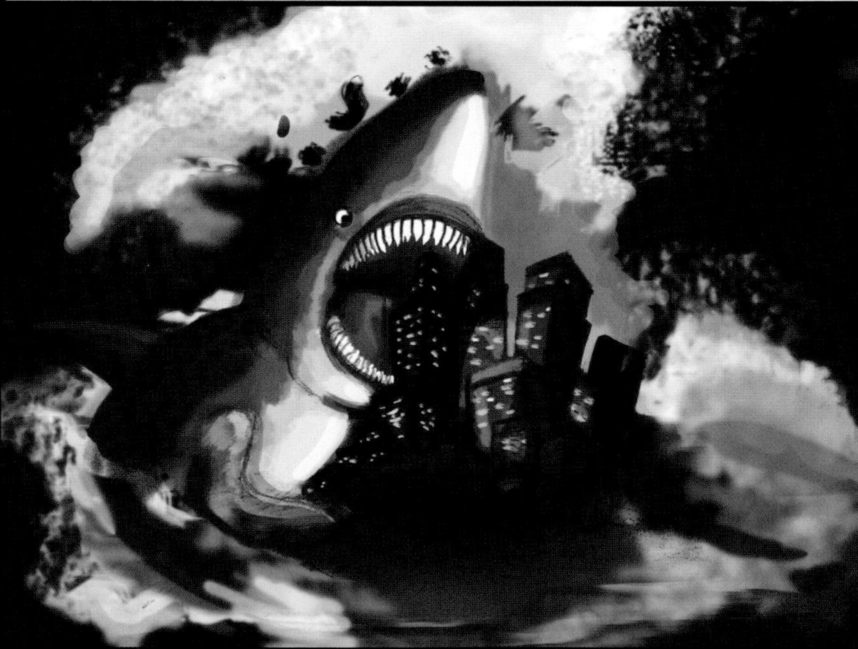

It's rare enough to see a shark picture that evokes warm, fuzzy feelings.

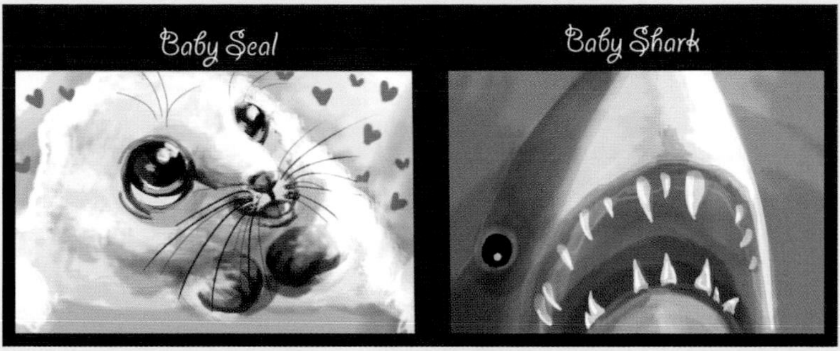
Baby Seal
Baby Shark

But since the entertainment industry continues depicting sharks as homicidal torpedoes with teeth...

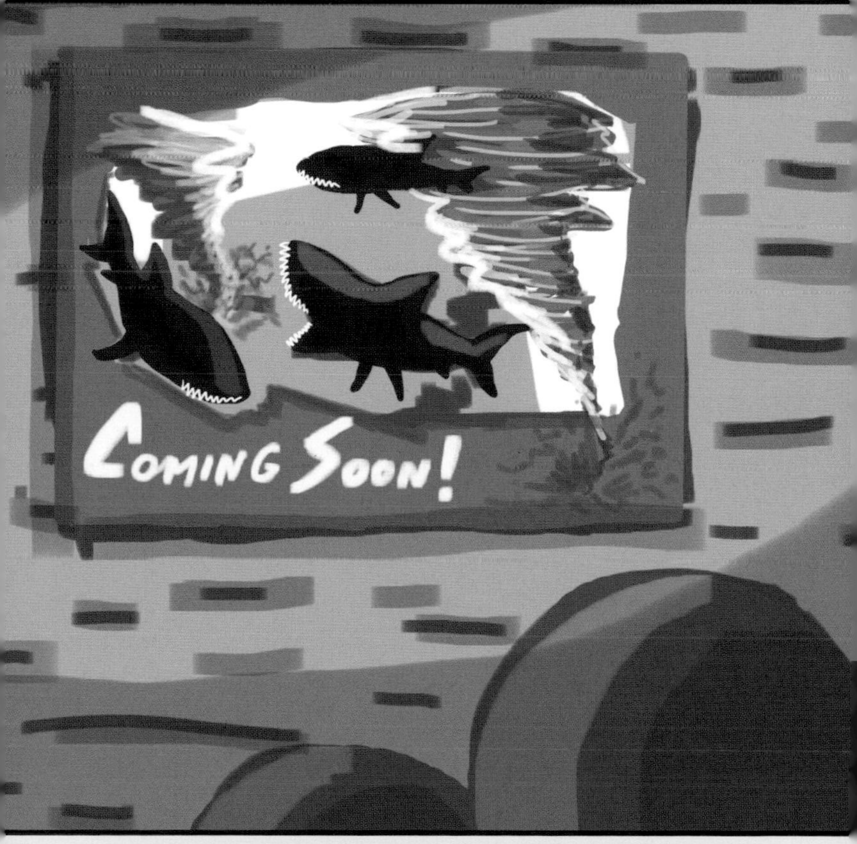
Coming Soon!

...galeophobia (fear of sharks) has taken hold in our society.

galeophobia
an abnormally large and persistent fear of sharks
* Insert bloodcurdling shriek *

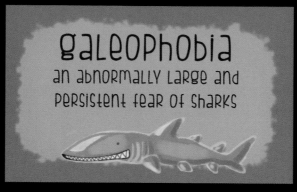

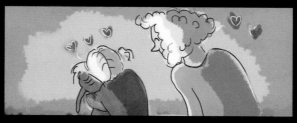

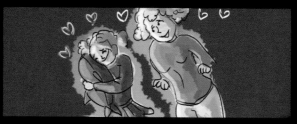

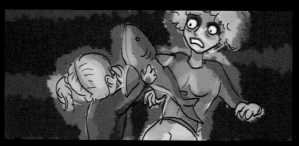

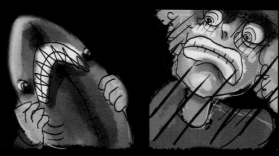

MYTH 1: SHARKS KILL PEOPLE BY THE GAZILLIONS

Statistically speaking, sharks are commonly found at the bottom of "number of people killed by animals" lists.

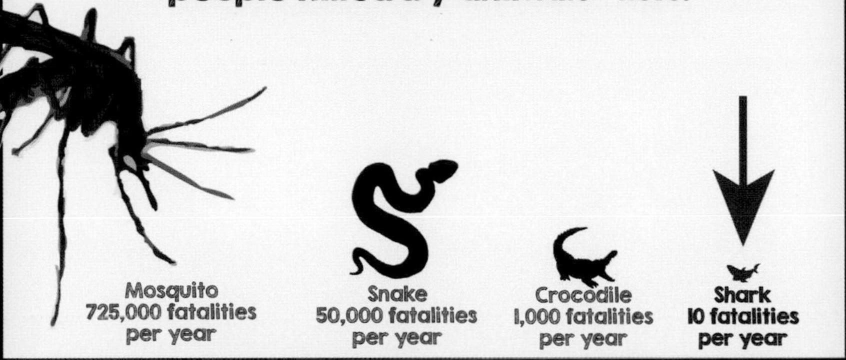
Mosquito
725,000 fatalities
per year
Snake
50,000 fatalities
per year
Crocodile
1,000 fatalities
per year
Shark
10 fatalities
per year

Cows kill about 22 people in the United States every year.

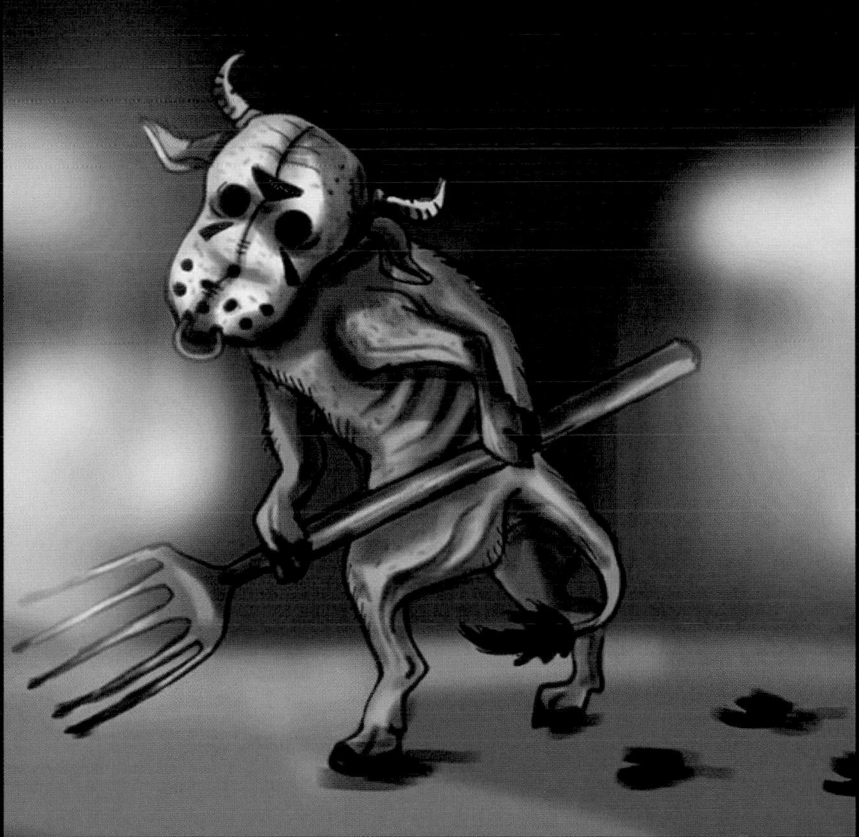

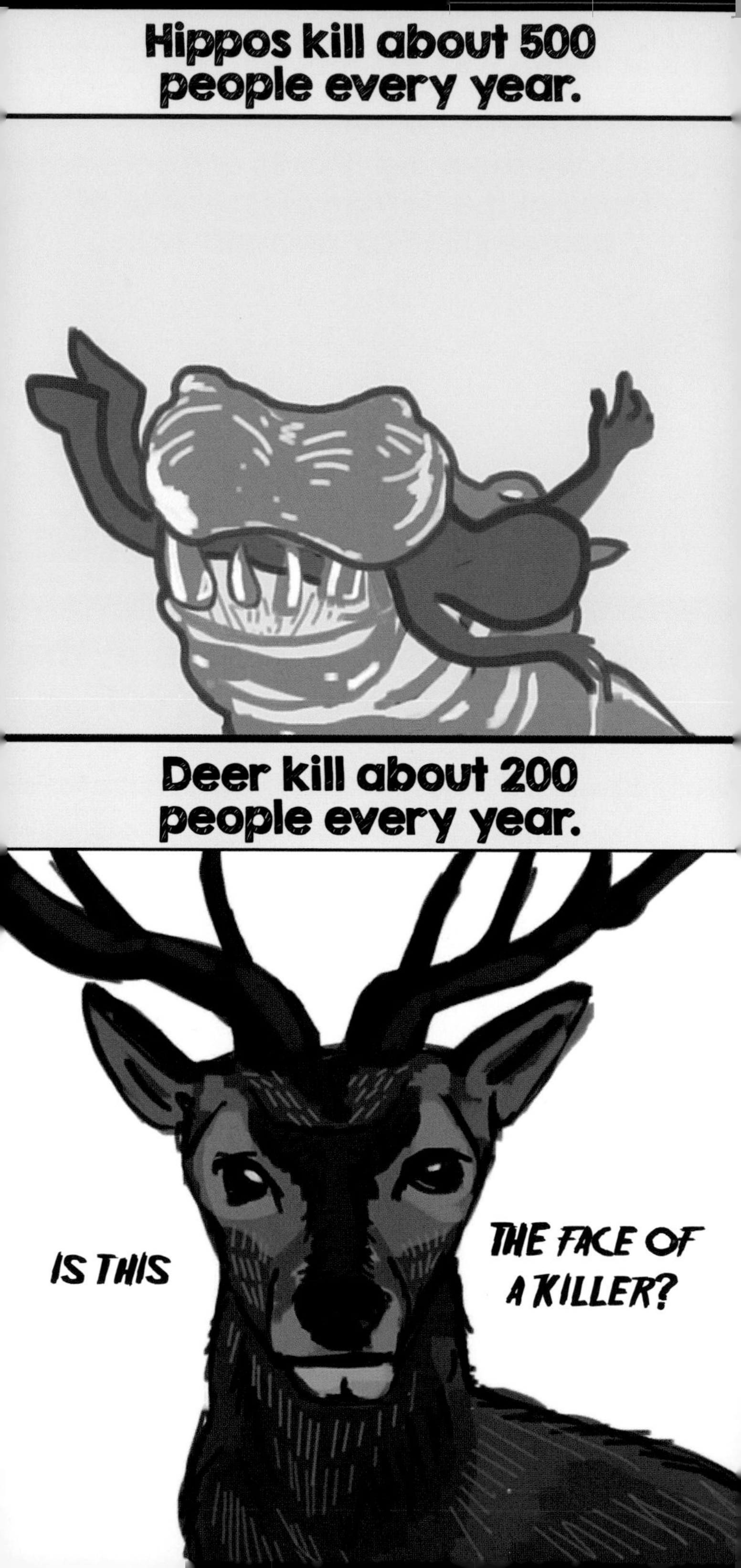
Hippos kill about 500 people every year.
Deer kill about 200 people every year.
IS THIS
THE FACE OF A KILLER?

From this, we can infer one of two possibilities:
1. Sharks are not interested in preying on humans.
Or
2. Sharks are really bad at hunting humans.

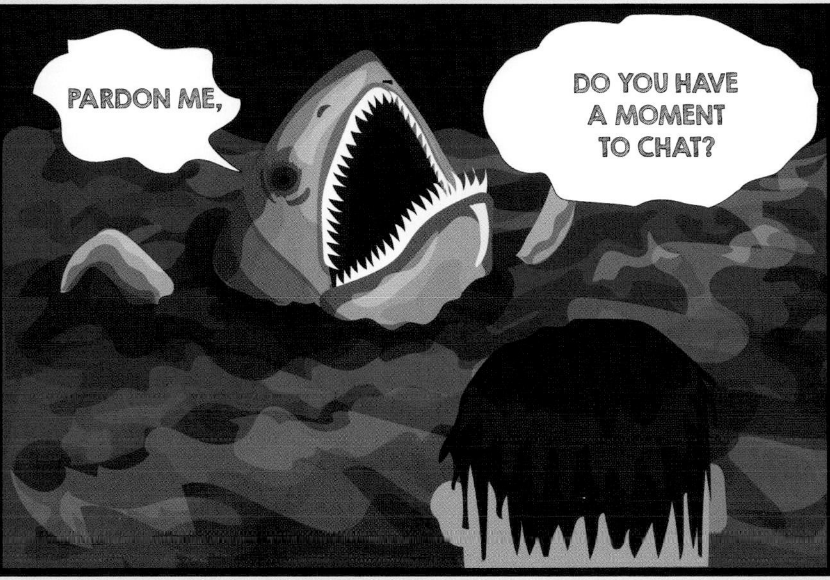
PARDON ME,
DO YOU HAVE A MOMENT TO CHAT?

MYTH 2: SHARKS PREY ON HUMANS

Although the idea of sharks disliking the taste of human flesh is debatable,

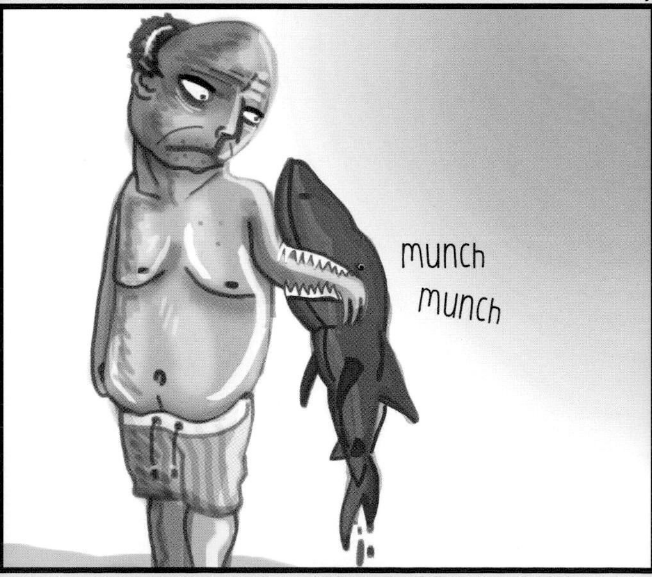
munch
munch

experts agree that sharks bite humans mainly out of curiosity.

So what do sharks mainly eat?

For great whites, it's seals.

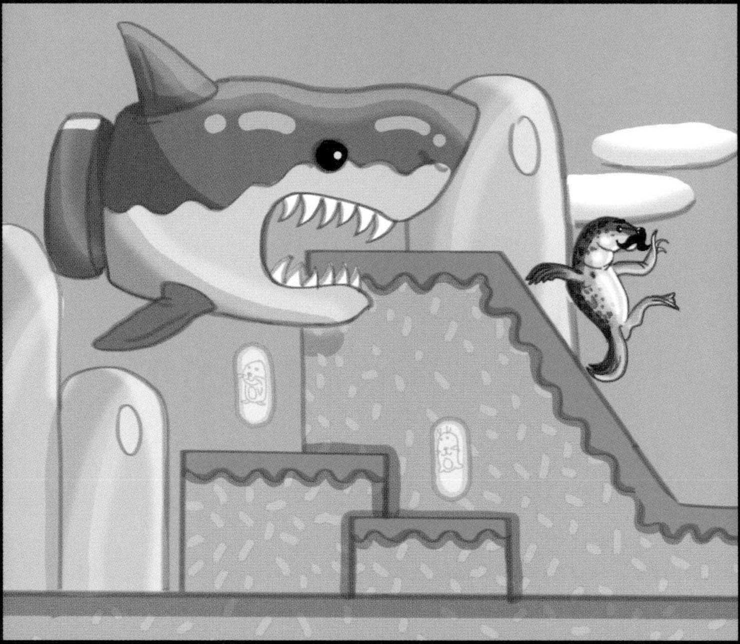

For whale sharks, it's plankton.

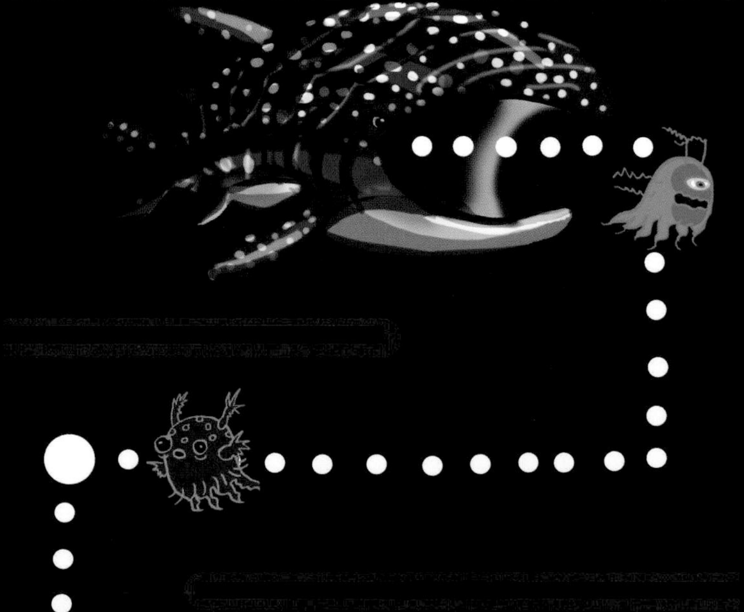

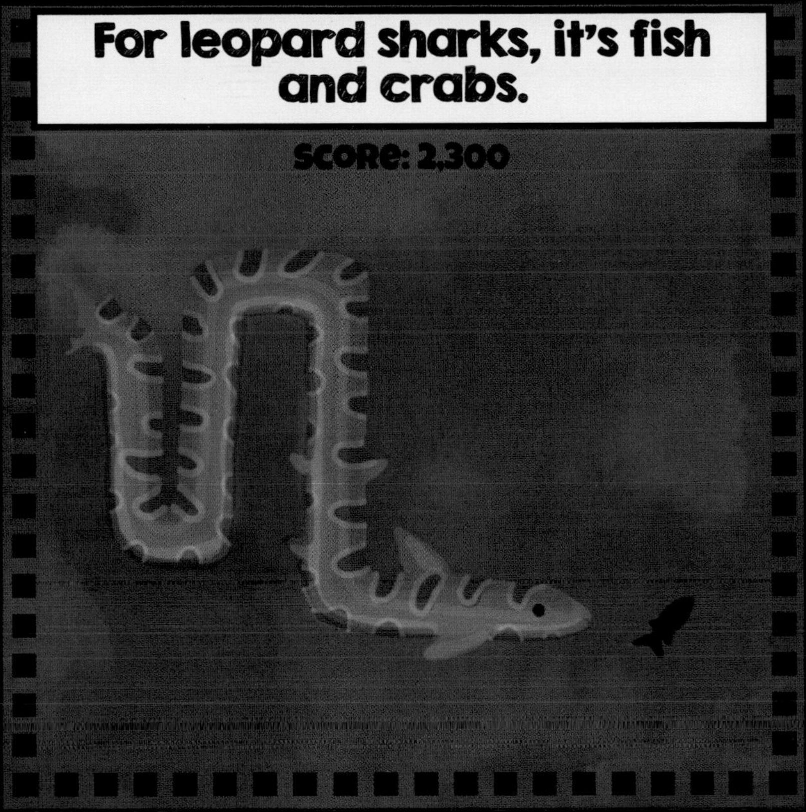
For leopard sharks, it's fish and crabs.
SCORE: 2,300

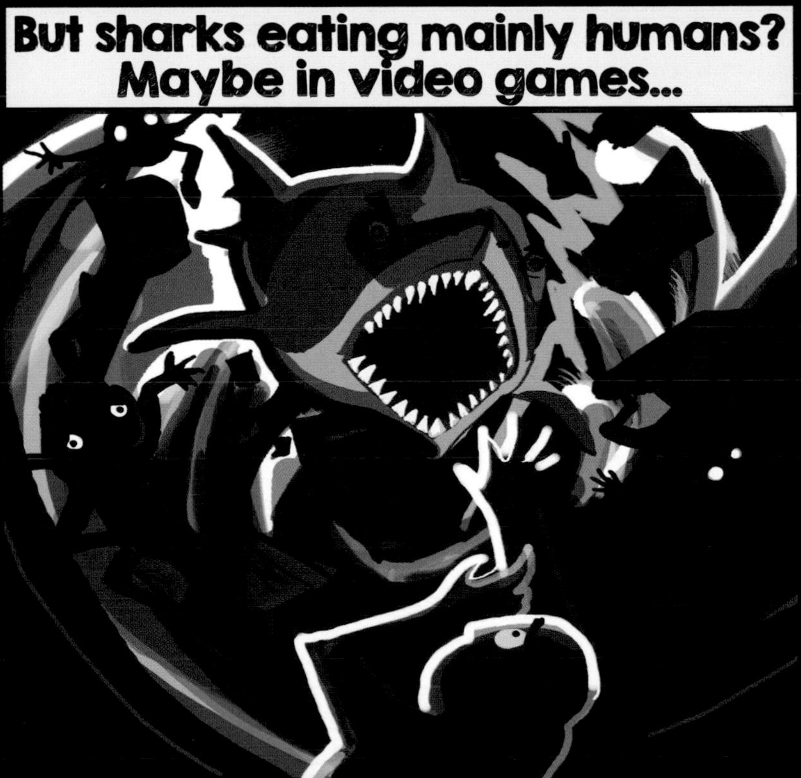
But sharks eating mainly humans? Maybe in video games...

MYTH 3: HUMANS ARE THE PRIMARY VICTIMS

Sharks kill

about 6 humans

per year.

Humans kill

63 to 273 million sharks

per year.

Assuming humans kill 100 million sharks in an average year, this amounts to 190 sharks killed per minute.

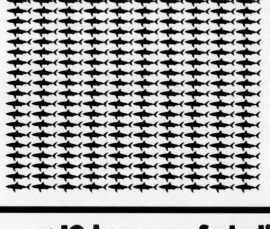

= 1 minute

If 10 human fatalities

per year are causing galeophobia,

then sharks must be

10 million times more traumatized

by anthropophobia (fear of humans).

anthropophobia
the fear of people
"Son, What are you doing??"
"Look, Pa! Look at what I found!"
"LOOK AT IT, POPS!!!!"
"IT'S SO WEIRD LOOKING!!!!!"....
* INSERT BLOODCURDLING SHRIEK *

CLOSING

Despite the underwhelming statistics,
shark attacks do occur.

However, it's unfair to label sharks as mindless
killing machines and resort to shark culling
just to feel safer.

Sharks play a vital role in keeping our oceans healthy.
Killing sharks threatens our fisheries and
our coral reefs.

Our hearts go out to the victims' families,
but we still need to keep things in perspective.

We simply cannot trade our fisheries and
remaining population of sharks for
a miniscule increase in safety.

Save our seals!

so our sharks can eat them.

Anatomy of the Giant Manta Ray

(a.k.a. the Majestic Sea Flap Flap)

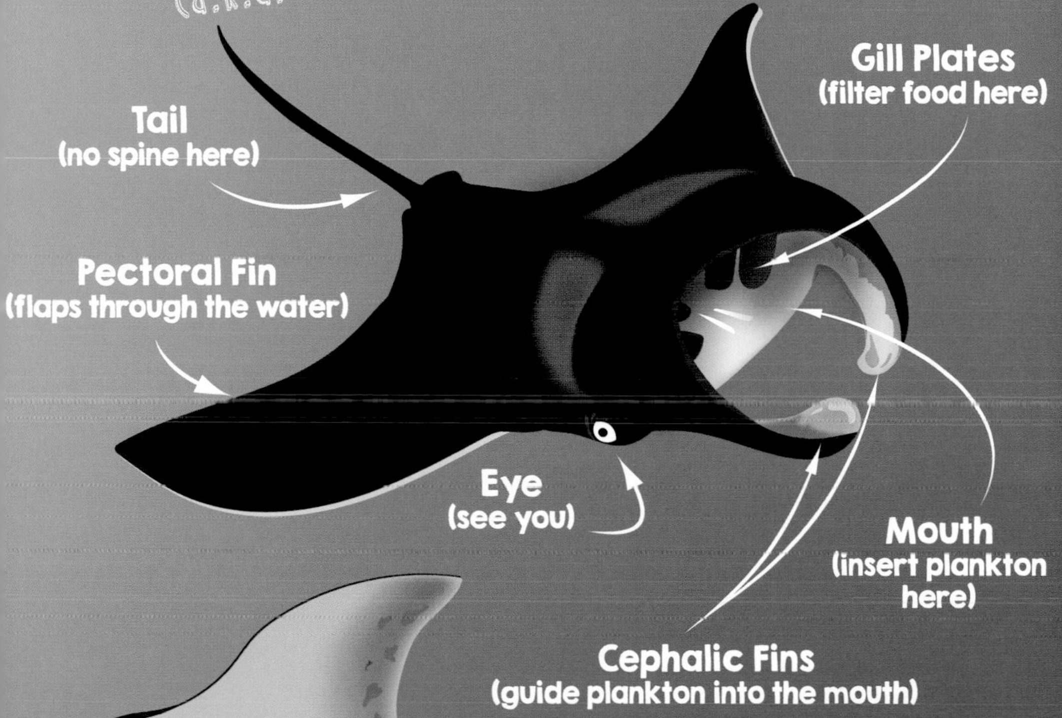
Gill Plates
(filter food here)
Tail
(no spine here)
Pectoral Fin
(flaps through the water)
Eye
(see you)
Mouth
(insert plankton here)
Cephalic Fins
(guide plankton into the mouth)

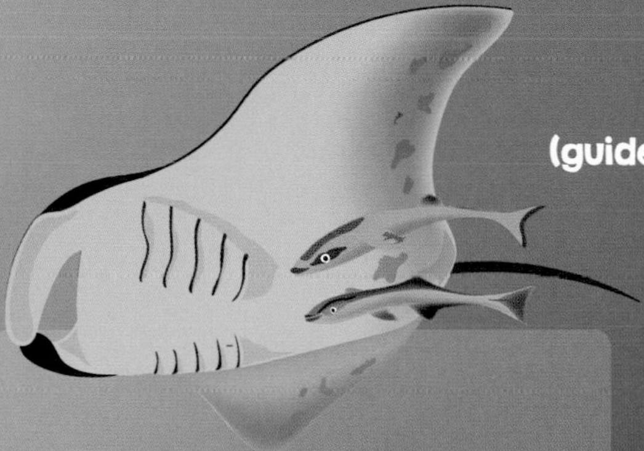

Hitchhikers of the Sea

Remoras latch onto large animals like the manta to get a free ride and free food. Fortunately, the suction doesn't hurt the manta.

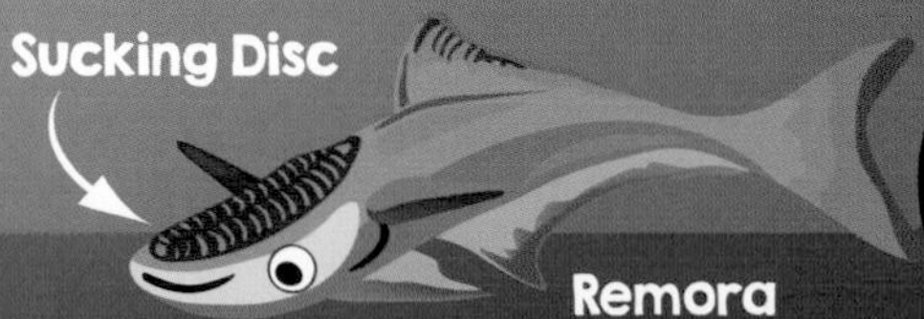
Sucking Disc
Remora

What's for Dinner?

Using their gill plates, manta rays filter the seawater for plankton to consume.

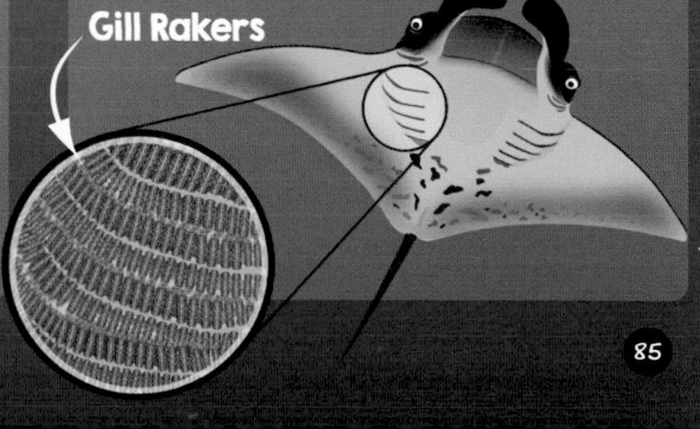
Gill Rakers

Anatomy of the Swell Shark

(inflates itself when threatened)

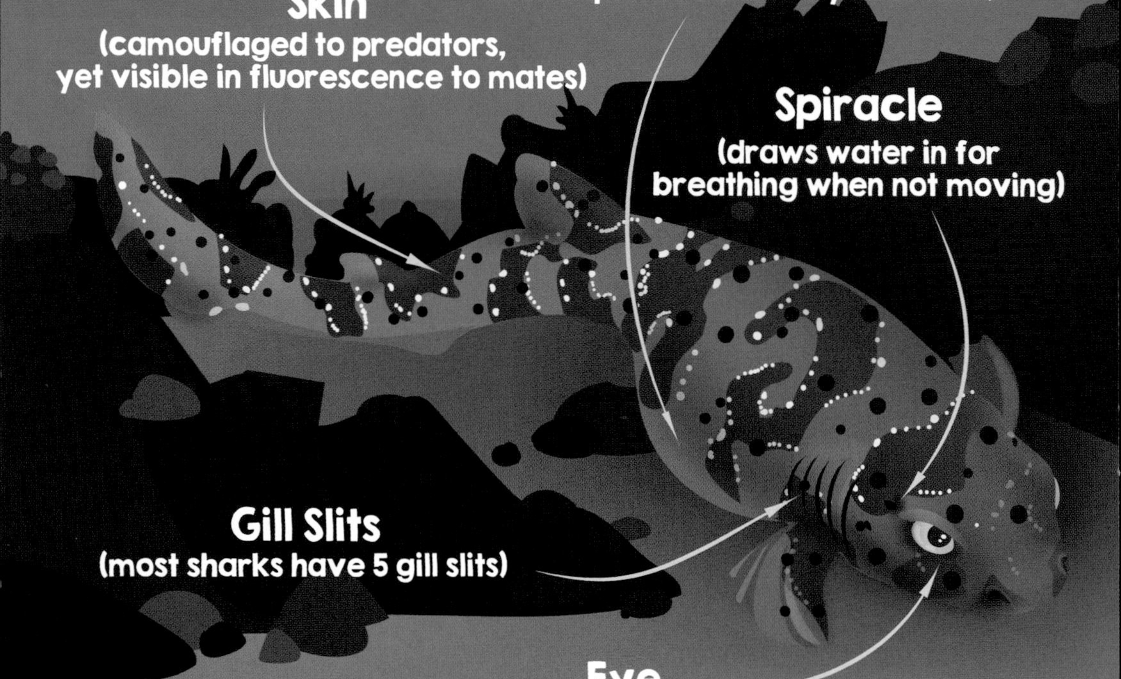
Inflatable Belly
(can expand its width by 2–3 times)
Skin
(camouflaged to predators, yet visible in fluorescence to mates)
Spiracle
(draws water in for breathing when not moving)
Gill Slits
(most sharks have 5 gill slits)
Eye
(yellow lens may help optimize fluorescence detection)

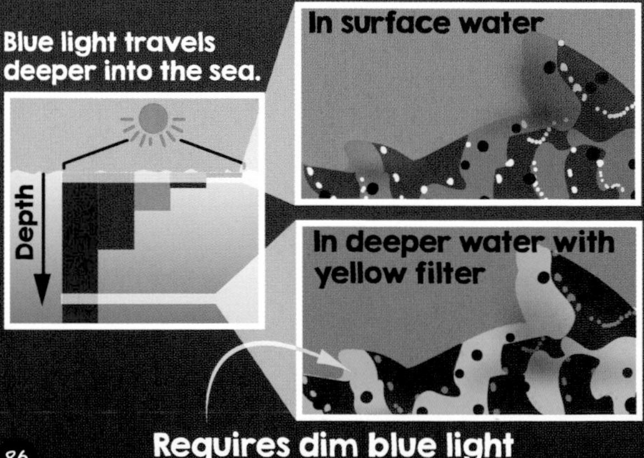
Blue light travels deeper into the sea.
Depth
In surface water
In deeper water with yellow filter
Requires dim blue light

Fluorescent Pattern

The spectrum of color diminishes with depth. Swell sharks live at a depth where mainly dim blue light is left. With its yellow lens and fluorescent skin, the swell shark can better identify its potential mates in a low-light environment.

What Is Fluorescence?

Fluorescence is the emission of light caused by the transformation of an external higher energy (different color) light source. This is not the same as "glow-in-the-dark" (or chemiluminescence) where emitted light is caused by a chemical reaction, not by an external light source.

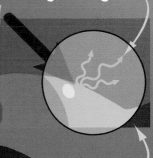

Deep ocean blue light

Emitted fluorescent green light

Yellow filter helps to distinguish fluorescent green from blue ambient light

Mermaid's Purse

Swell sharks lay their eggs in kelp and rocky crevices to keep them from hungry animals. It can take 9–12 months before the shark hatches.

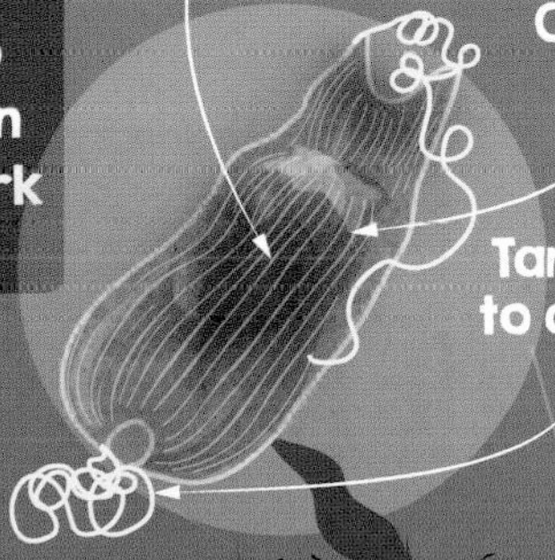

Baby swell shark

Color blends with kelp

Tangles in kelp to anchor itself

Inflates When Threatened

Swell sharks aren't the biggest fish around! When threatened by another hungry fish, the swell shark will hide in a crevice, inflate itself, and stay wedged inside to avoid being lunch.

Inflates its stomach with seawater

SHARKTUNES:
How Background Music Affects Your Perception of Sharks

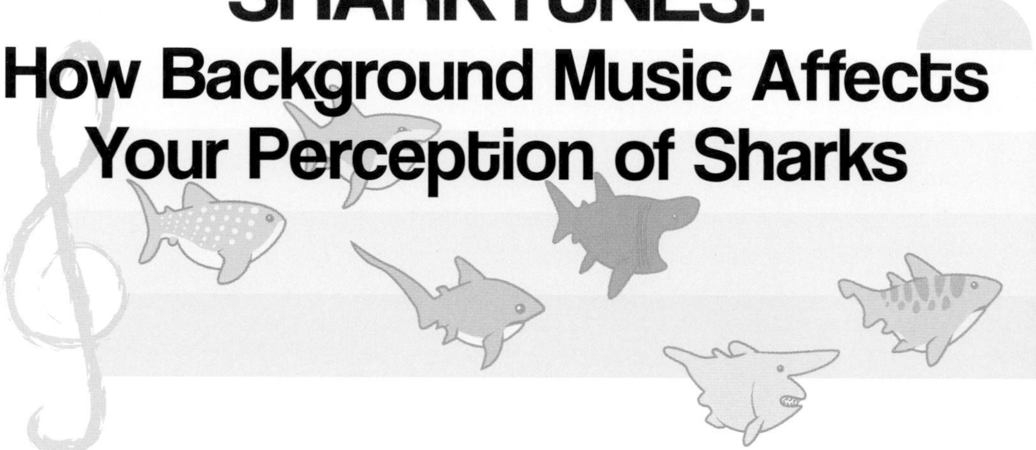

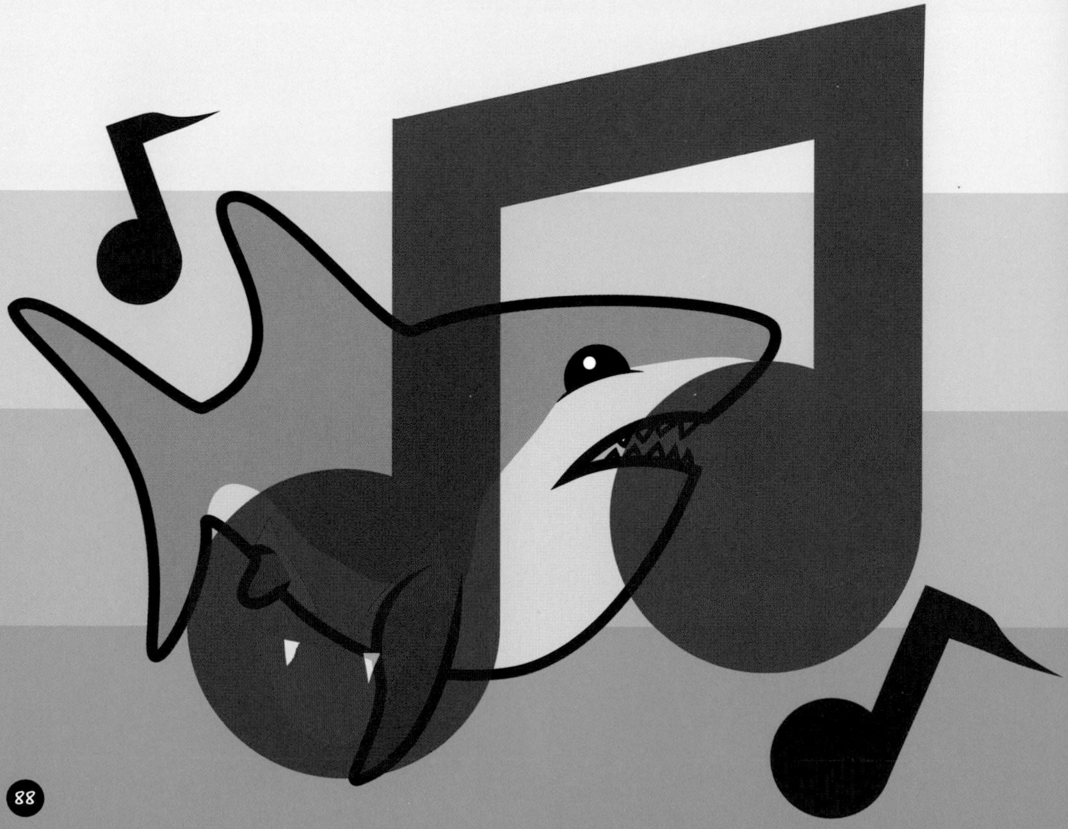

Global shark populations have declined due to overfishing, finning (the practice of removing a shark's fins), and habitat degradation.

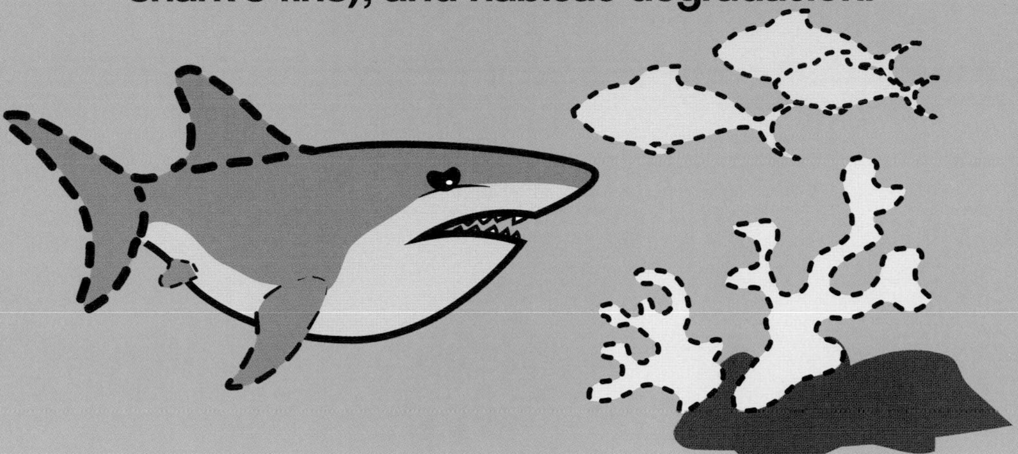

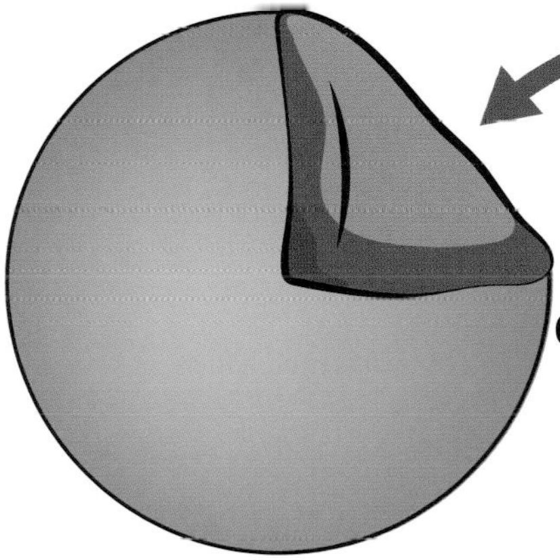

In fact, one quarter of sharks and related species are currently listed as threatened with extinction (IUCN).

International public opinion is changing, and support to protect sharks is growing.

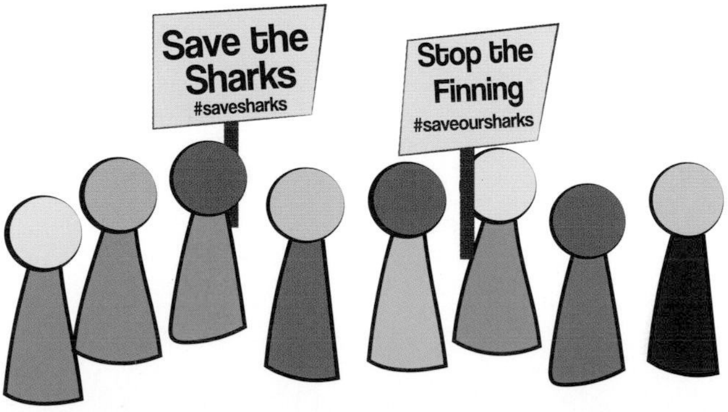
Save the Sharks
#savesharks
Stop the Finning
#saveoursharks

However, our instinctive yet exaggerated fear of sharks (galeophobia) continues to be exploited for cheap media thrills.

NOW SHOWING

Sharknadocano
Plus Hail

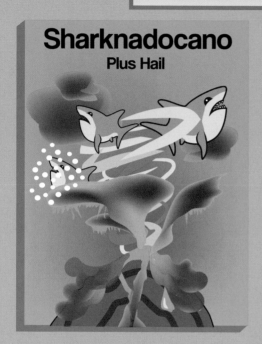

The Tidepools
Shallower than the Shallows

A recent study investigated how our perception of sharks is affected by background music.

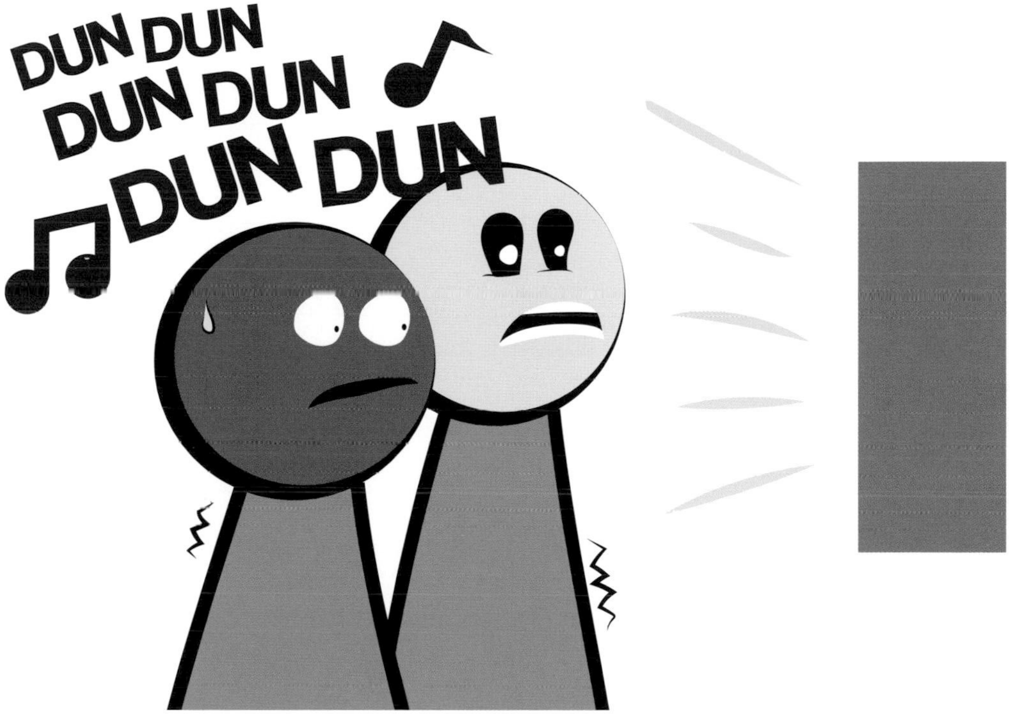
DUN DUN
DUN DUN
DUN DUN

Participants were shown the same video clip of sharks swimming with one of three background music clips playing.

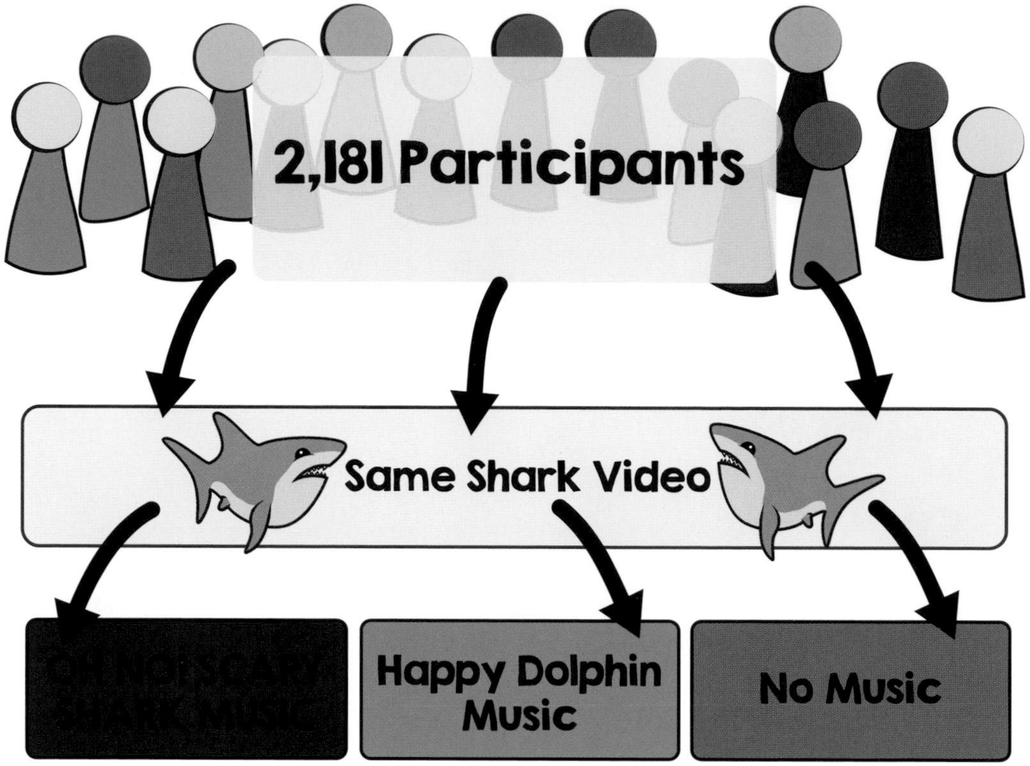
2,181 Participants
Same Shark Video
[redacted]
Happy Dolphin Music
No Music

Scientists found that the participants' reactions to the sharks were significantly affected by the background music they were given.

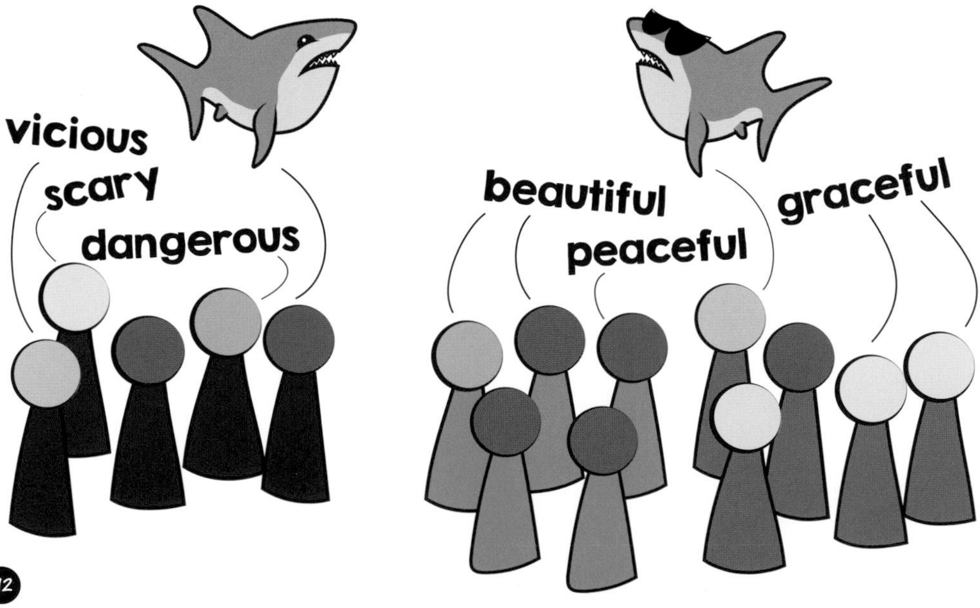
vicious
scary
dangerous
beautiful
peaceful
graceful

ANATOMY OF THE Moon Jelly

(no heart, brain, lungs, or bones)

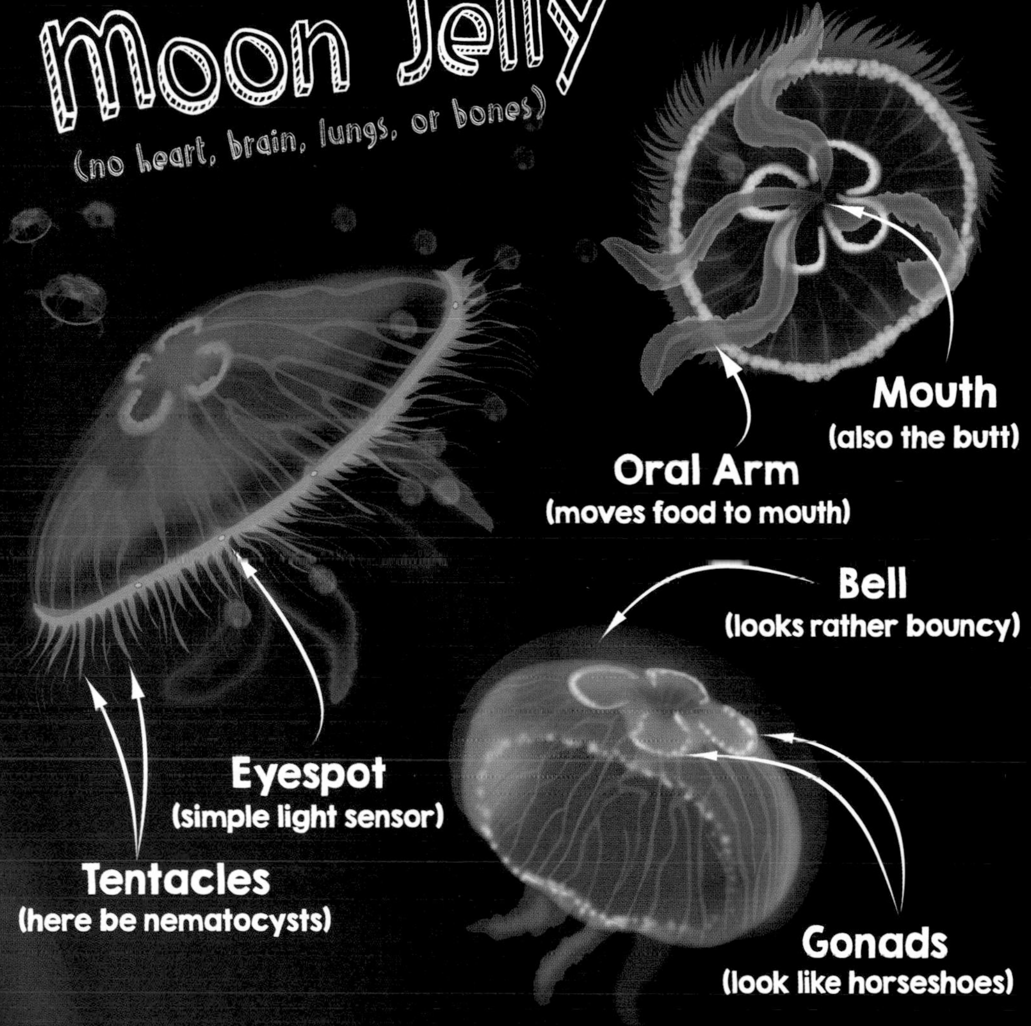

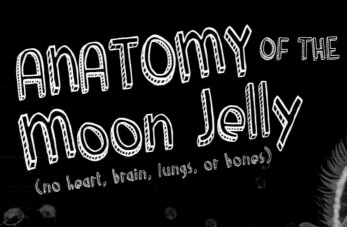

Mouth
(also the butt)
Oral Arm
(moves food to mouth)
Bell
(looks rather bouncy)
Eyespot
(simple light sensor)
Tentacles
(here be nematocysts)
Gonads
(look like horseshoes)

Bombs Away!

Moon jellies use special cells called nematocysts to sting and stun their prey. Once fired, the cells will need to be replaced.

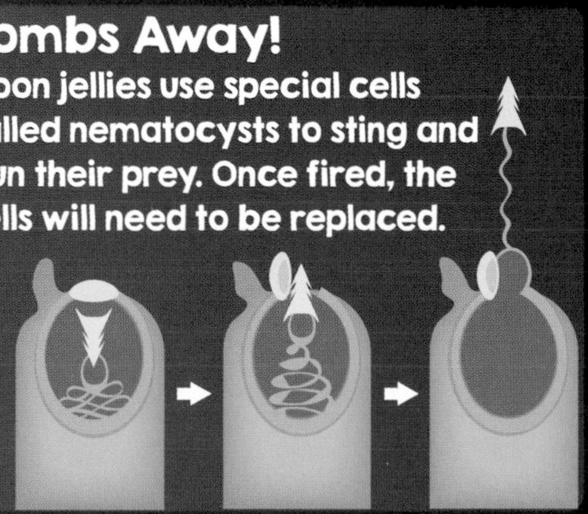

Sea ~~Jelly~~ Water

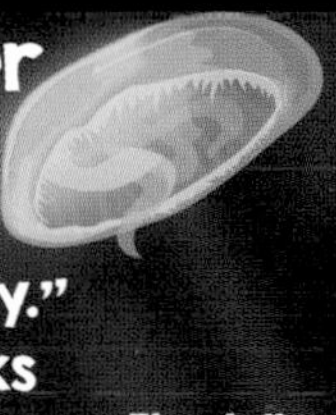

Like other sea jellies, moon jellies are 95% seawater and 5% "jelly." This is why a jelly looks like a blob when out of the water.

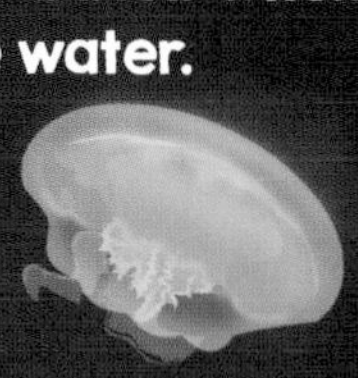

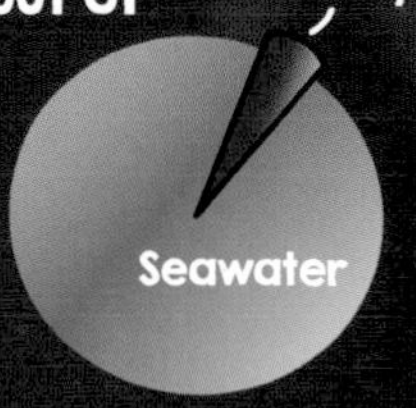

The Jelly
Seawater

ANATOMY OF THE
Velella velella
(commonly called by-the-wind sailor)

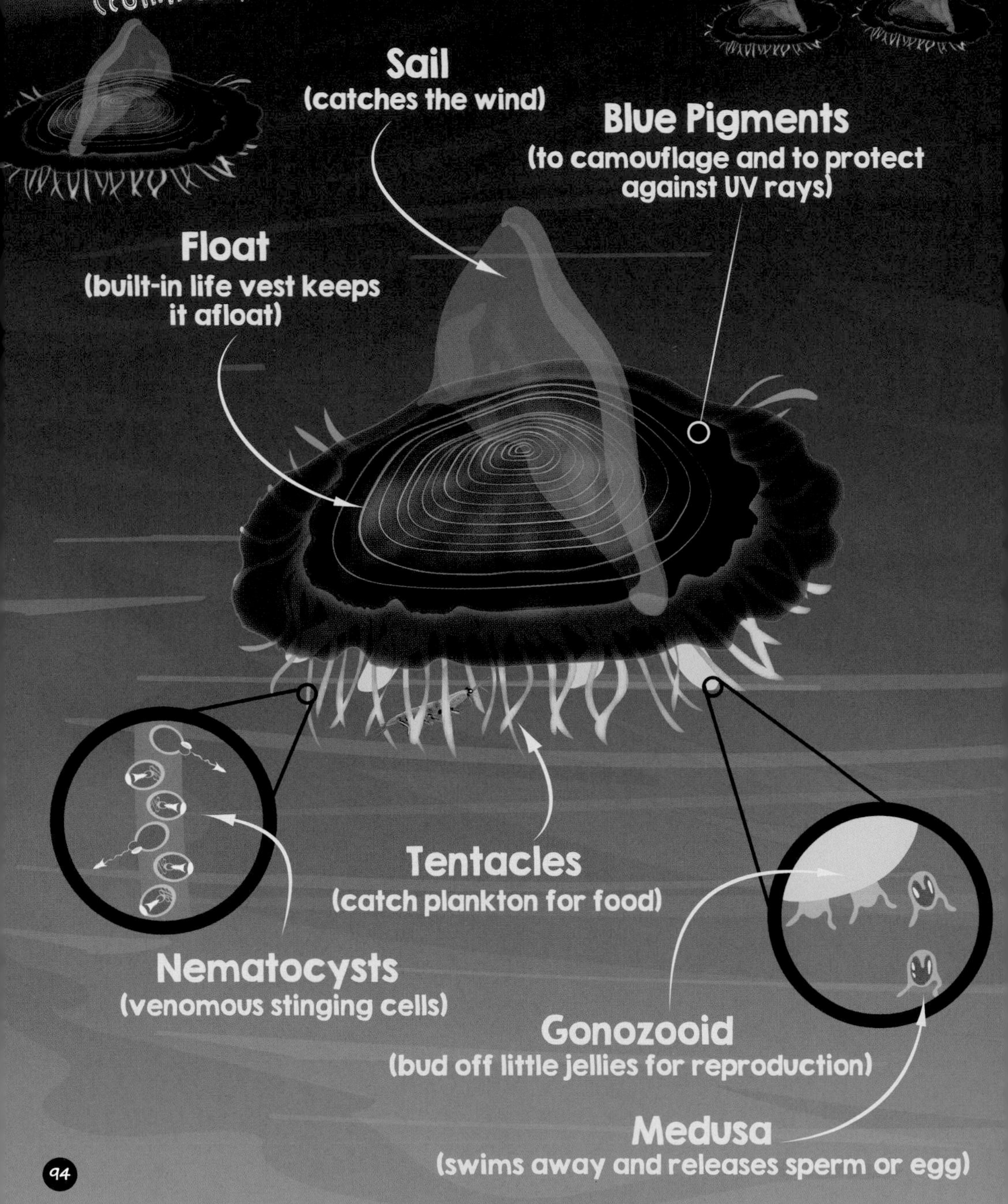

Sail
(catches the wind)

Blue Pigments
(to camouflage and to protect against UV rays)

Float
(built-in life vest keeps it afloat)

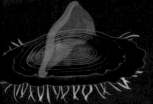

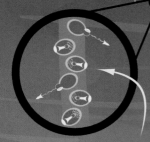

Tentacles
(catch plankton for food)

Nematocysts
(venomous stinging cells)

Gonozooid
(bud off little jellies for reproduction)

Medusa
(swims away and releases sperm or egg)

Team Fortress of Stingers

The *V. velella* may look like one organism, but it is actually a colony of organisms called zooids, each playing a specific role.

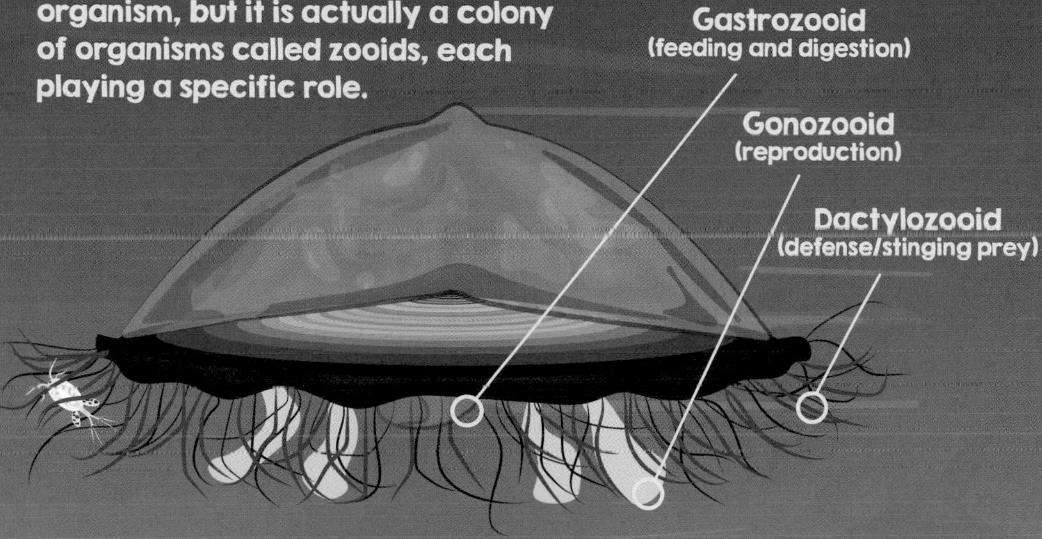

Gastrozooid
(feeding and digestion)

Gonozooid
(reproduction)

Dactylozooid
(defense/stinging prey)

Life Is a Crash Course

V. velella is fully dependent on the wind and currents for movement. On occasion, strong winds and currents can cause mass *V. velella* strandings.

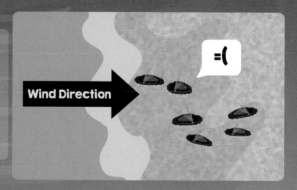

Wind Direction

=(

POISONOUS vs. VENOMOUS
Explained with Mugs

Poisonous: capable of causing harm or death when taken into the body

Examples: cane toad, poison dart frog, milkweed butterfly

POISONOUS
Touched
Ingested
Inhaled

POISONOUS vs. VENOMOUS
Explained with Mugs

Venomous: **capable of injecting toxin by means of biting or stinging**

Examples: blue-ringed octopus, wasp, jellyfish, platypus

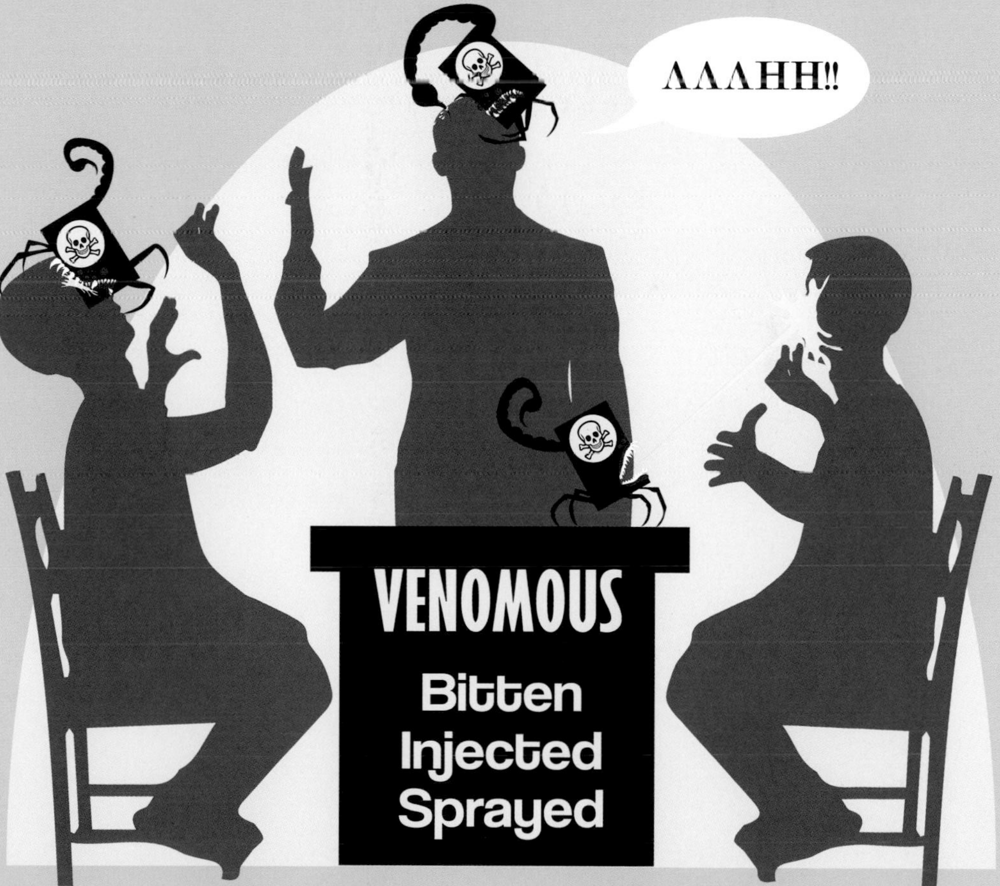
AAAHH!!
VENOMOUS
Bitten
Injected
Sprayed

Note: No mugs were harmed in the making of this comic.

ANATOMY OF THE Green Sea Turtle

(that's not always green)

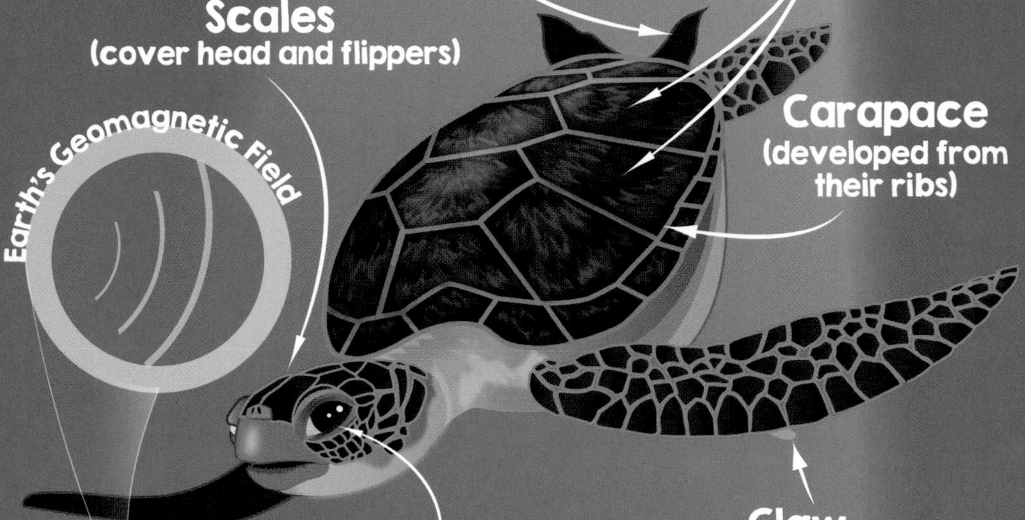
Scutes
(bony plates that make up the carapace)
Tail
(males have larger tails than females)
Scales
(cover head and flippers)
Earth's Geomagnetic Field
Carapace
(developed from their ribs)
Claw
(males use it to hold onto females during mating)
Eyes
(natural nearsightedness helps with underwater vision)

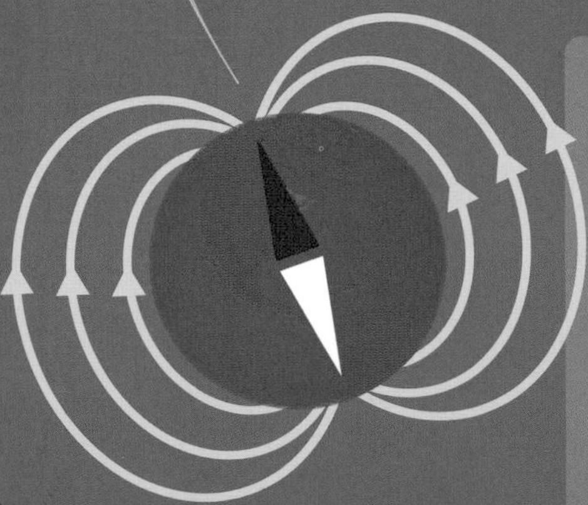

Geomagnetic Compass

Sea turtles sense the earth's magnetic field, and females may use this ability to navigate back to their natal beaches to mate and lay eggs. This internal magnetic compass functions as a guide for journeys that span thousands of miles to and from egg-laying and feeding grounds.

A Changing Diet

Young green turtles eat crabs, snails, and other small animals. Most adult green turtles eat a strict diet of algae and seagrasses.

Diet Turns Turtles Green

This diet of marine plants turns the fat under the carapace green, which gives this sea turtle its name.

Juvenile

Adult

Sea Turtle Age

Key Difference Between Male and Female Turtles

One big difference between male and female green sea turtles is the length of their tail. The tail of male turtles will extend past their carapace, while the tail of female turtles will not extend past their shell (assuming the turtles are at least 25–30 years old).

Female

Male

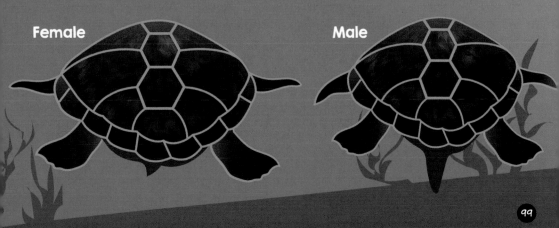

Anatomy of the Narwhal

(originally meant "corpse whale")

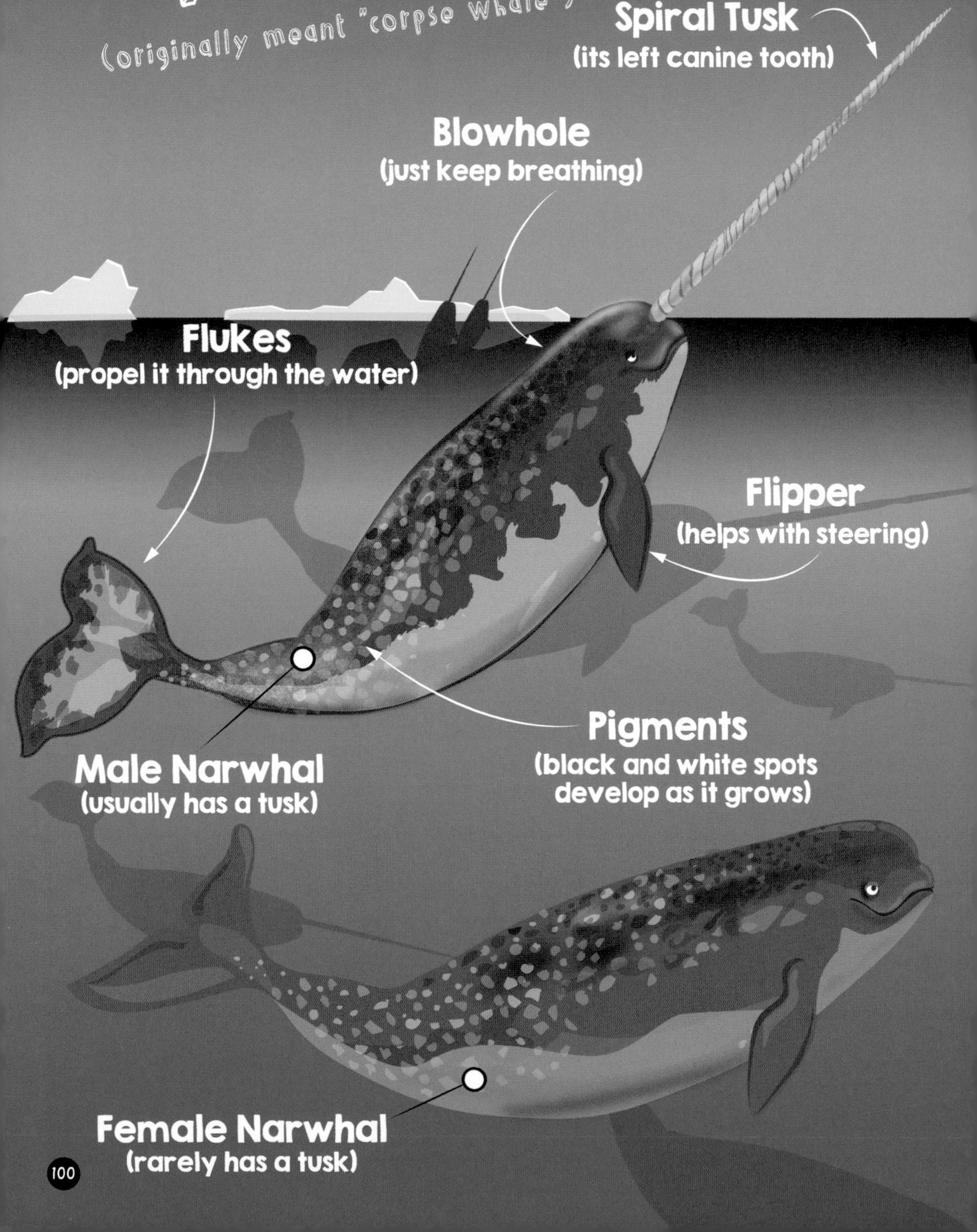

Spiral Tusk
(its left canine tooth)
Blowhole
(just keep breathing)
Flukes
(propel it through the water)
Flipper
(helps with steering)
Pigments
(black and white spots develop as it grows)
Male Narwhal
(usually has a tusk)
Female Narwhal
(rarely has a tusk)

Toothless Eating

The narwhal has two teeth, but neither are used for feeding. Instead, narwhals create a vacuum in their mouth and slurp up their food. Recently, there has been evidence showing that narwhals use their tusks to stun fish before eating them.

SMACK

The amount of salt in the water

Possible Salinity Detector?

Scientists recently discovered that the narwhal's tusk is porous and has a network of sensory cells and nerves. While this may suggest the tusk is used for detecting salt concentration in water, most scientists think the tusk is used for mating selection.

Scientists argue the tusk cannot serve a critical role for survival because female narwhals, most of which lack a tusk, manage to thrive and live longer than male narwhals.

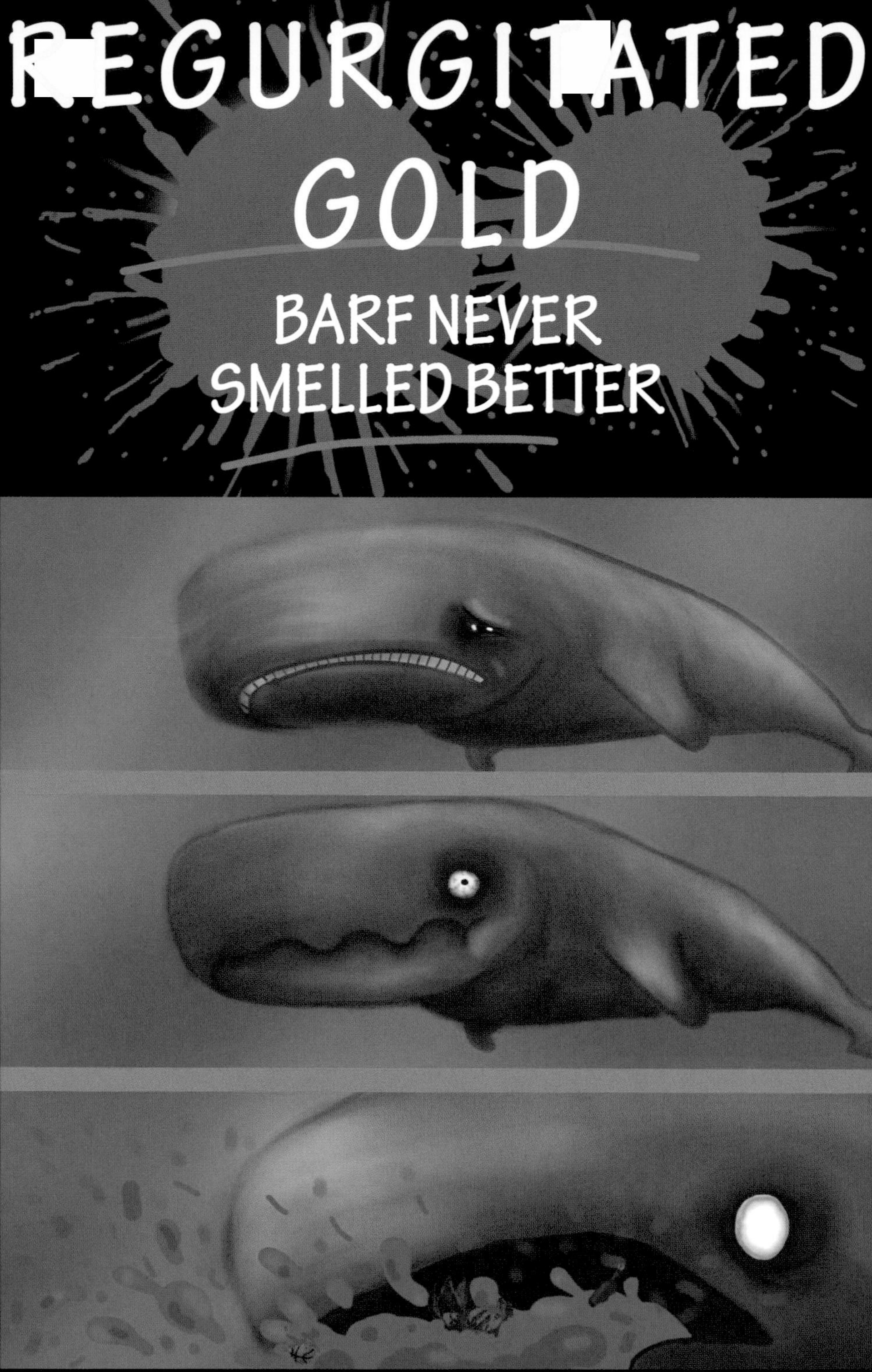
REGURGITATED
GOLD
BARF NEVER
SMELLED BETTER

SPERM WHALES

THROW UP ROUTINELY.

Some claim it's for digestive reasons....

Others may blame seasickness....

Whatever the case,
THERE ARE ACTUALLY PEOPLE IN THIS WORLD
WHO GO OUT OF THEIR WAY
TO COLLECT

WHALE VOMIT

(also called ambergris).

CAPTAIN, What's green and smells REALLY GOOD??
MONEY??

BUT WAIT.

Here's a plot twist:

AMBERGRIS, A.K.A. WHALE VOMIT,
DOES HAVE REAL VALUE.

However silly the concept of "valuable vomit"

may seem,

whale vomit has been
considered an important resource
throughout history, and still
is today—

because it contains chemical properties

that only the wisest of

WIZARD WHALES

can concoct ....

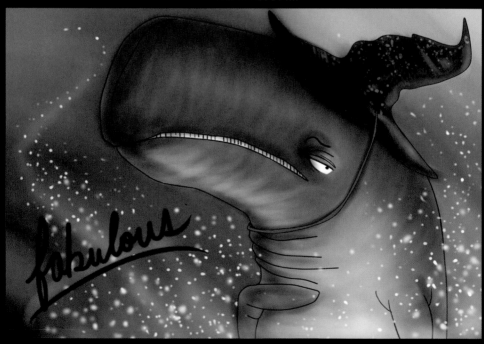

fabulous

Just think: Coming upon some whale vomit is like finding a winning lottery ticket.

Currently, **just a couple pounds of vomit could go for**

$100,000

(give or take).

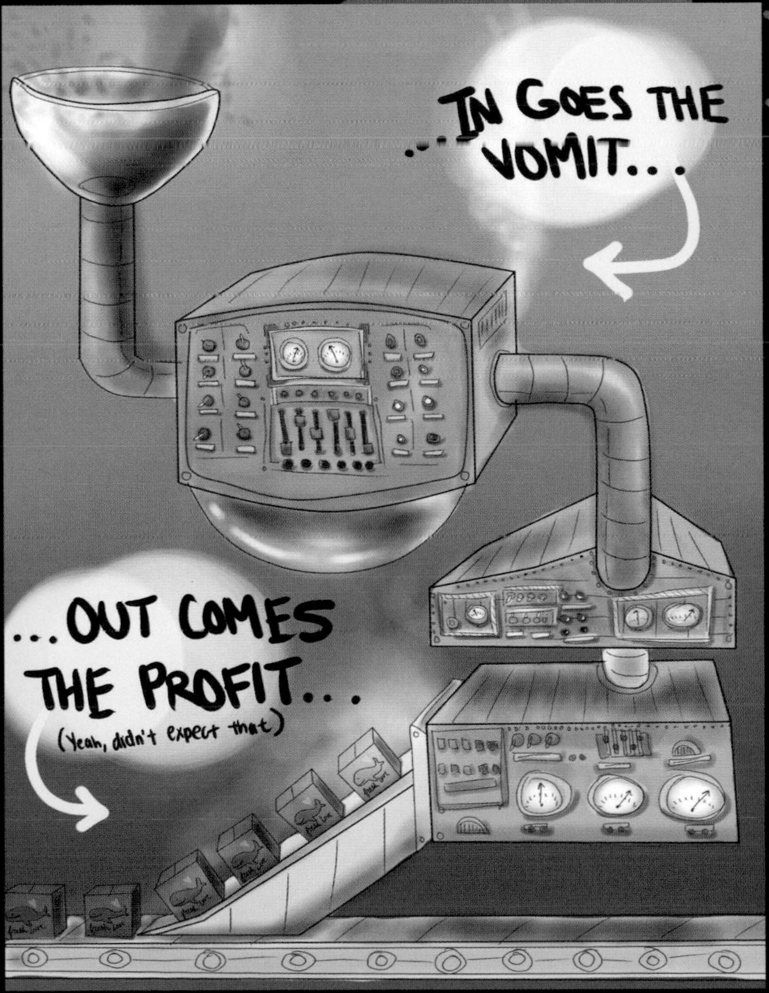
...IN GOES THE VOMIT...
...OUT COMES THE PROFIT...
(Yeah, didn't expect that)

So who or what exactly drives this demand for HALF-DIGESTED UPCHUCK, you may ask?

(HINT: IT'S AN ANSWER ANYONE COULD SNIFF OUT. HEHEHE.)

THE

PERFUME

INDUSTRY

WANTS YOUR WHALE VOMIT, AND IT WANTS IT NOW.

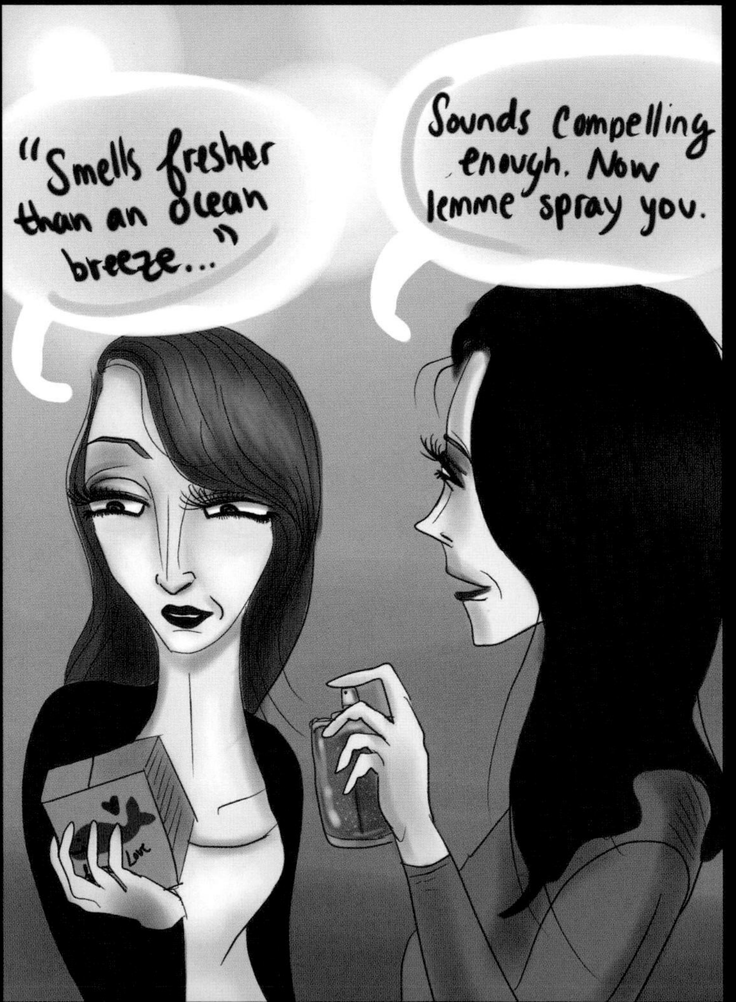
"Smells fresher than an ocean breeze..."
Sounds compelling enough. Now lemme spray you.

That's right.

Perfumes, body mists, and colognes are often made using

WHALE VOMIT.

That fancy perfume your grandma wears?
It just might have had its humble beginnings

IN THE BELLY OF A SPERM WHALE.

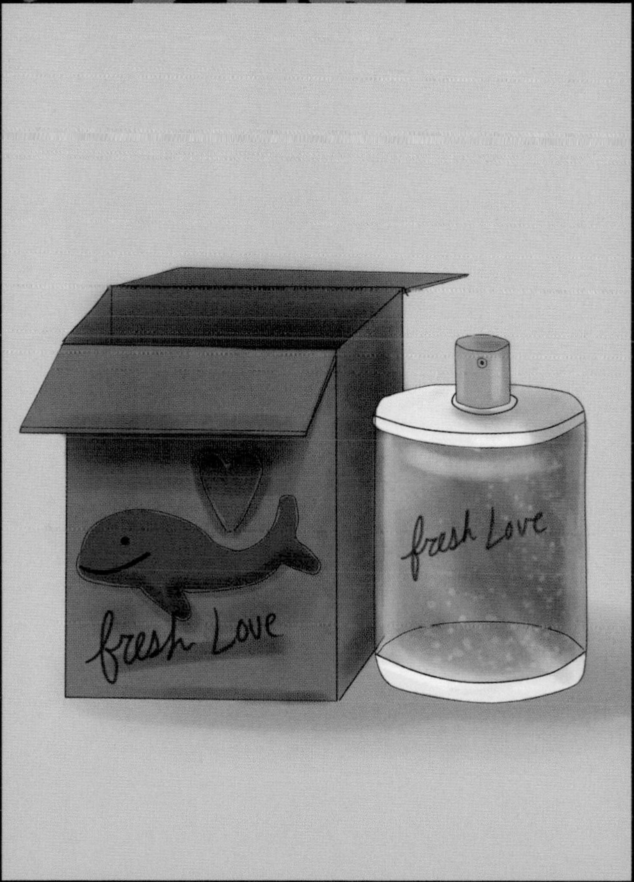

fresh Love
fresh Love

Anatomy of the Leptocephalus

(the larval stage of many types of eels)

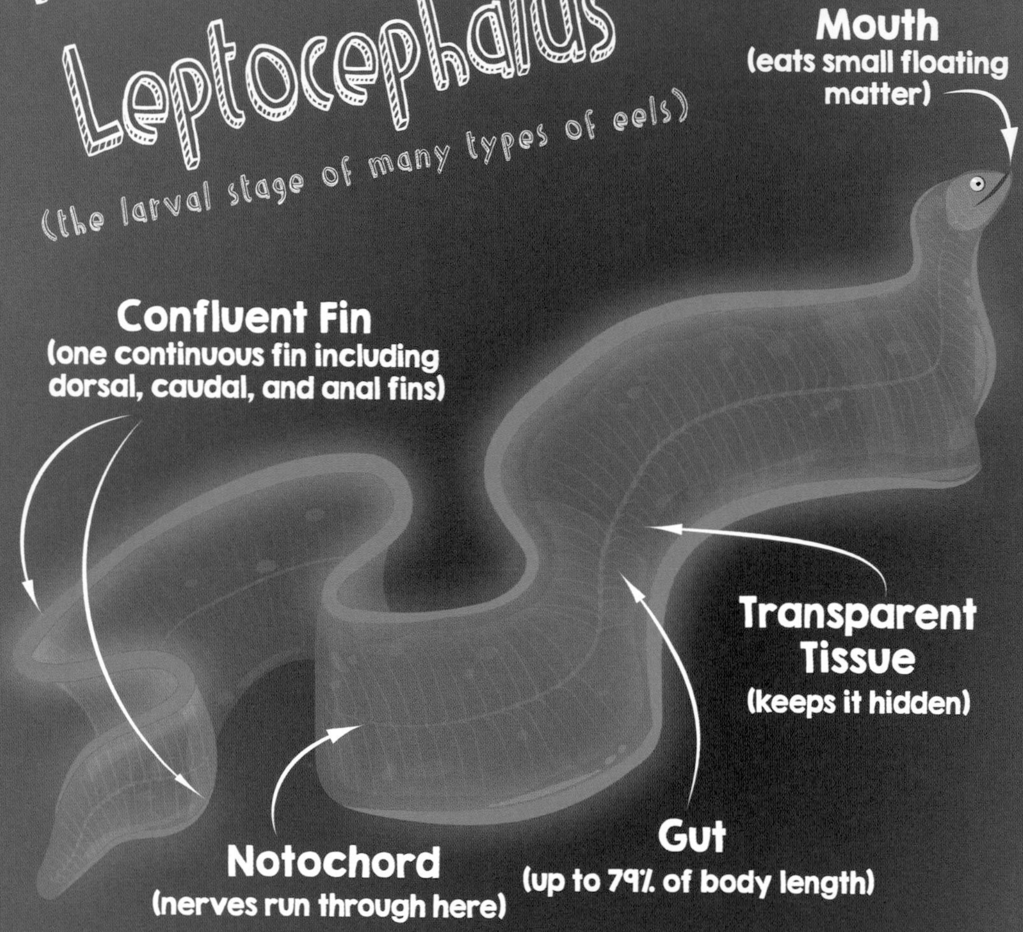
Mouth
(eats small floating matter)
Confluent Fin
(one continuous fin including dorsal, caudal, and anal fins)
Transparent Tissue
(keeps it hidden)
Gut
(up to 79% of body length)
Notochord
(nerves run through here)

European Eel Life Cycle

Leptocephalus is just one stage in the eel's life cycle. Thanks to the currents surrounding the Sargasso Sea, the eel moves around the ocean as it grows.

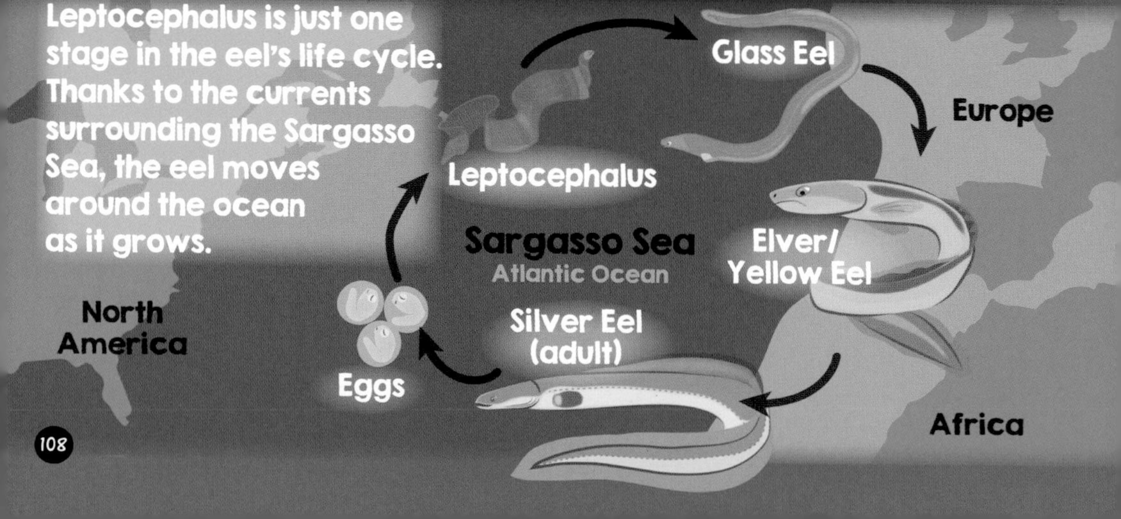
Glass Eel
Europe
Leptocephalus
Sargasso Sea
Atlantic Ocean
Elver/
Yellow Eel
North
America
Silver Eel
(adult)
Eggs
Africa

Embryo Stage

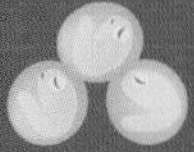

The eggs of the European eel develop as they drift in the currents. Many eggs drift west with the north equatorial current.

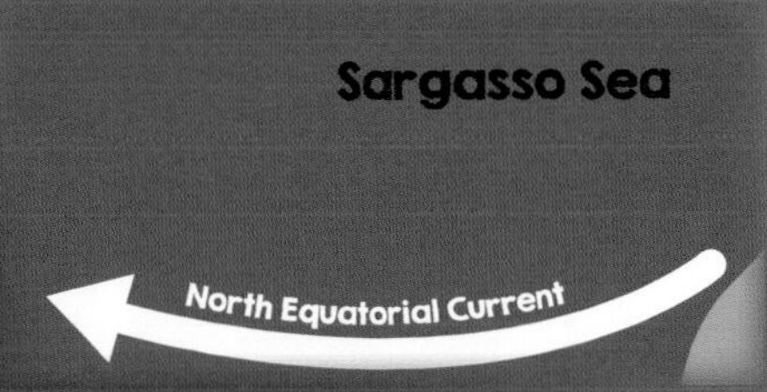
Sargasso Sea
North Equatorial Current

Larval Stage

To avoid being fish food, the leptocephalus camouflages itself with its nearly transparent flesh. It even postpones making red blood cells until later in development.

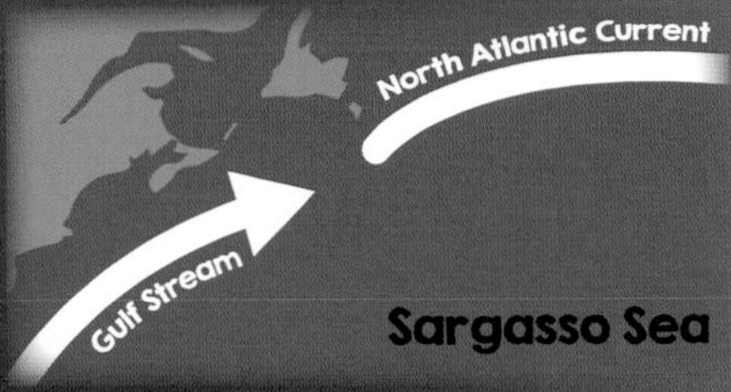
North Atlantic Current
Gulf Stream
Sargasso Sea

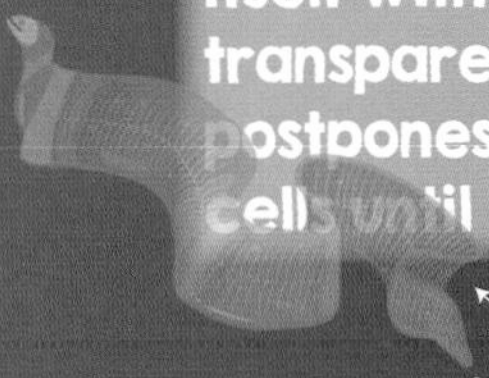
YOU CAN SEE THROUGH IT!

Early Juvenile Stage

The leptocephalus slowly develops a more eellike body. At this point, it is known as the glass eel. The glass eel then starts swimming into freshwater areas, where it begins forming pigments and becomes known as the elver.

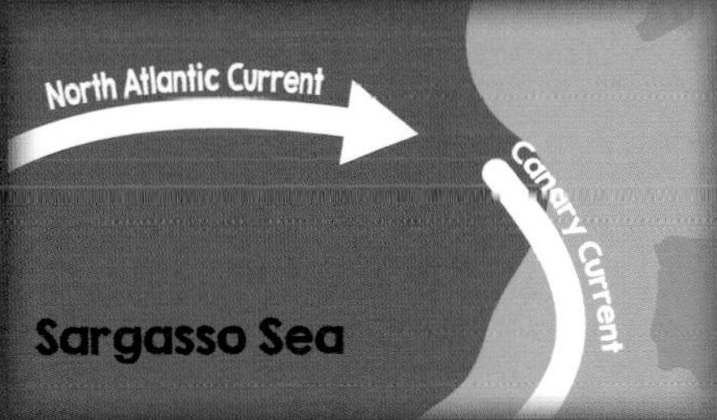
North Atlantic Current
Canary Current
Sargasso Sea

Later Juvenile Stage

Once the yellow pigments fully cover the eel, it becomes known as the yellow eel. It continues to feed in the freshwater rivers and coastal ocean until it is ready for mating.

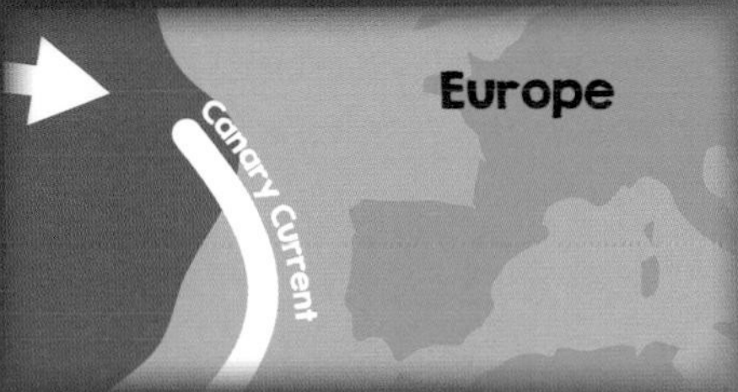
Europe
Canary Current

Spawning Adult Stage

When the eel is ready to mate, it turns silvery in color and is called the silver eel. It swims back to the ocean and dives deeper to mate. However, this is a one-way trip, as the eel dies shortly after spawning.

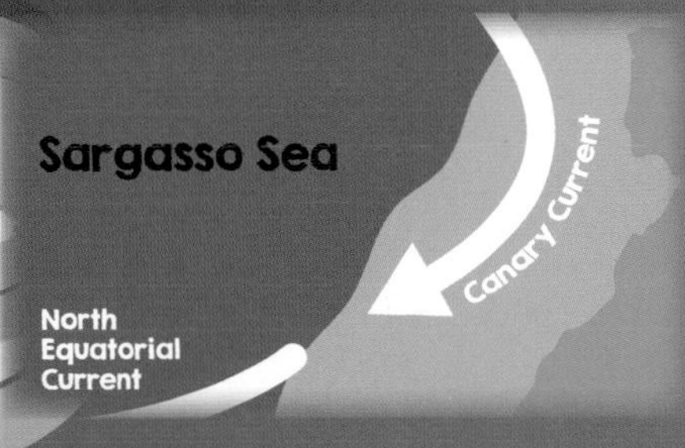
Sargasso Sea
Canary Current
North Equatorial Current

ANATOMY OF THE Coral Polyp

(tiny animals, huge reefs)

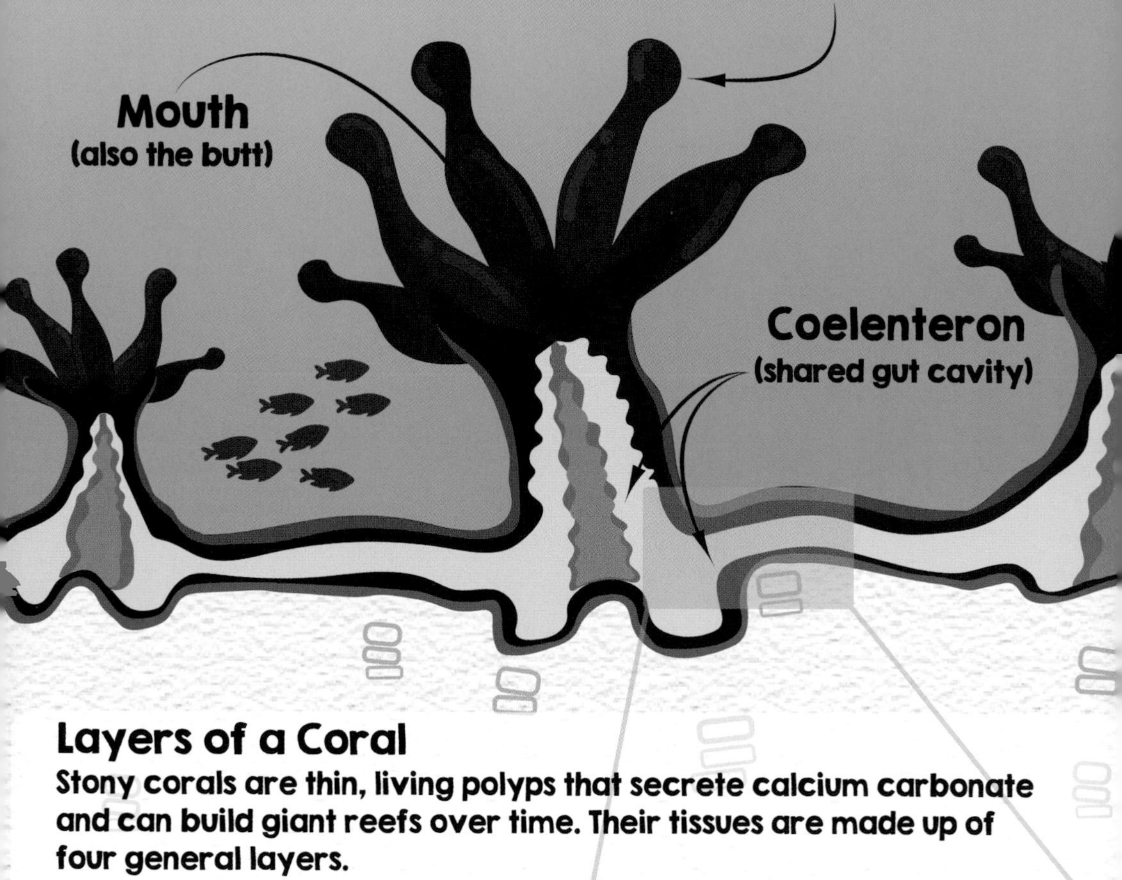

Tentacle
(grabs plankton from the water)
Mouth
(also the butt)
Coelenteron
(shared gut cavity)

Layers of a Coral

Stony corals are thin, living polyps that secrete calcium carbonate and can build giant reefs over time. Their tissues are made up of four general layers.

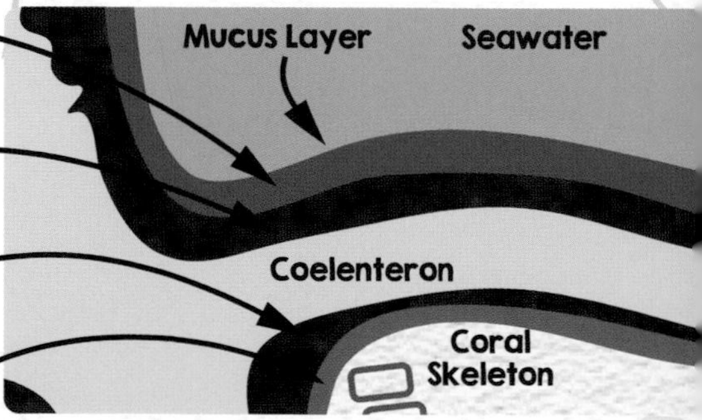

Oral Ectoderm
(has nematocysts; produces mucus that protects coral from UV rays and more)
Oral Endoderm
(houses the *Symbiodinium*)
Aboral Endoderm
(also houses the *Symbiodinium*)
Aboral Ectoderm
(secretes the coral skeleton)
Mucus Layer
Seawater
Coelenteron
Coral Skeleton

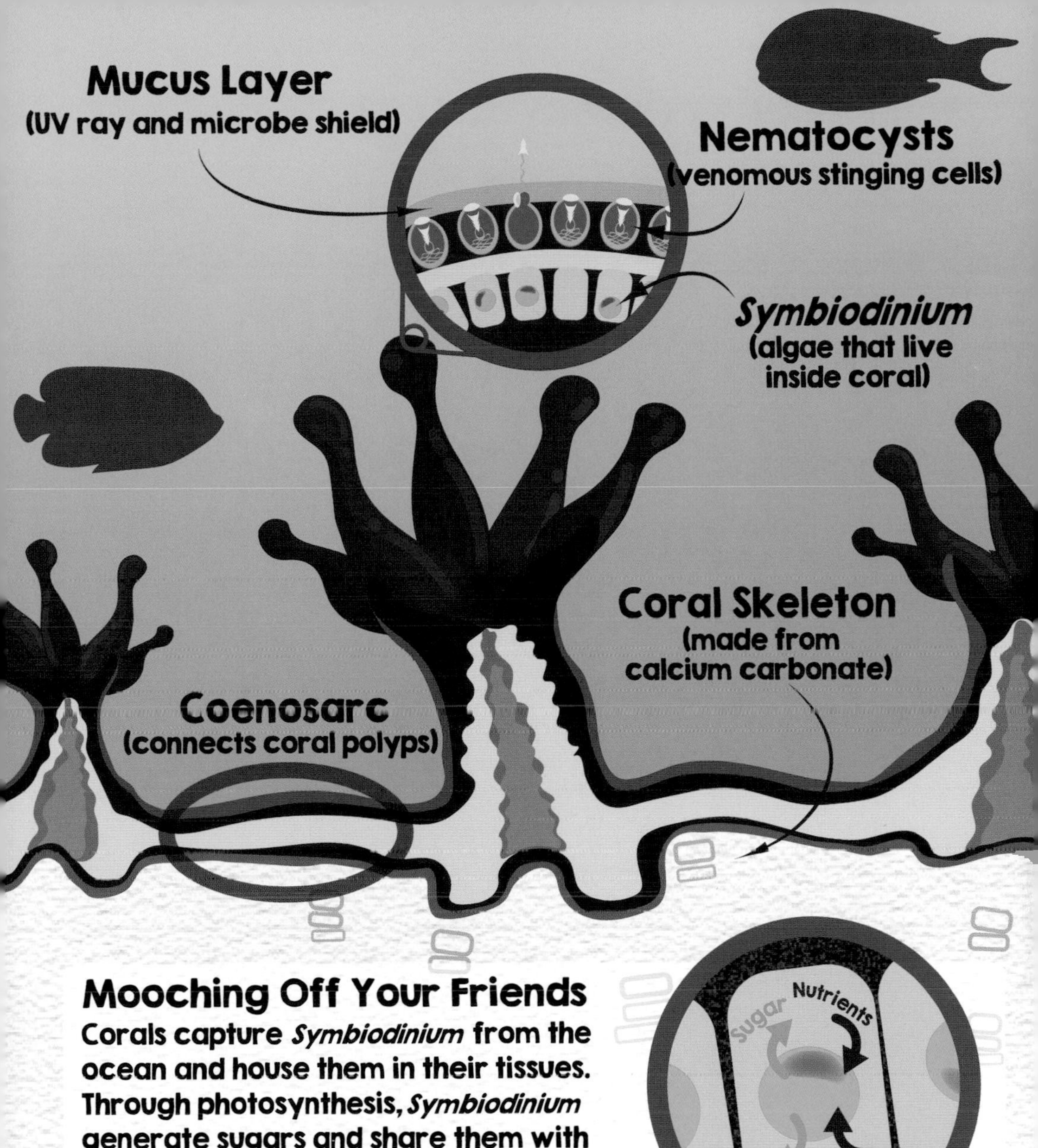
Mucus Layer
(UV ray and microbe shield)
Nematocysts
(venomous stinging cells)
Symbiodinium
(algae that live inside coral)
Coral Skeleton
(made from calcium carbonate)
Coenosarc
(connects coral polyps)

Mooching Off Your Friends

Corals capture *Symbiodinium* from the ocean and house them in their tissues. Through photosynthesis, *Symbiodinium* generate sugars and share them with the coral. In return, the coral provides the algae with a home and with nutrients needed for photosynthesis.

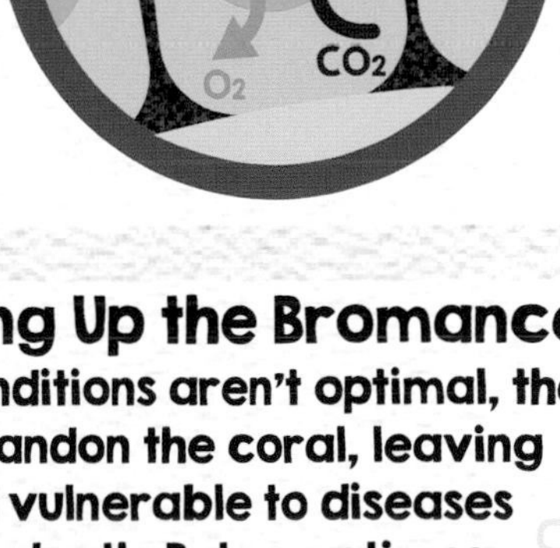
Sugar
Nutrients
O_2
CO_2

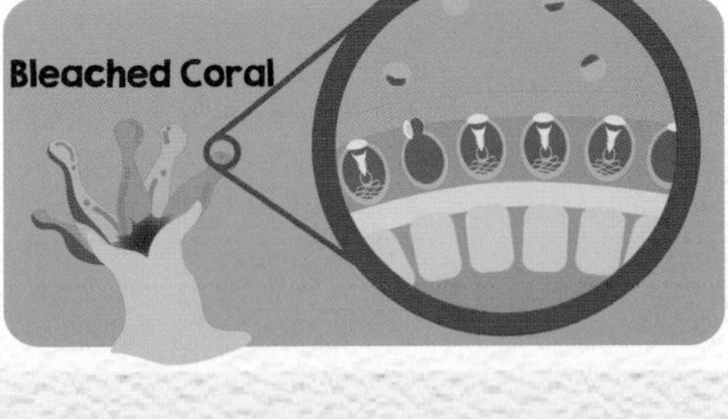
Bleached Coral

Breaking Up the Bromance

When conditions aren't optimal, the algae abandon the coral, leaving the coral vulnerable to diseases and even death. But sometimes the coral can take up new algae when conditions improve.

Sea Lions vs. Seals:
Can You Tell Them Apart?

Physical Differences

SEA LION

SEAL

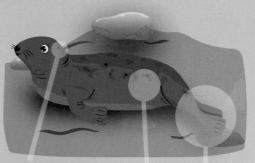

External ear flaps

Has fur and blubber

Hind flippers can rotate forward to walk on all fours

Lacks external ear flaps

Mostly blubber, little fur

Hind flippers cannot rotate forward, so it scoots on its belly

How They Swim

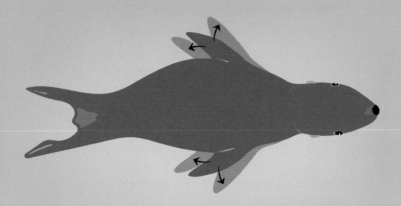

Sea lions swim using their forward flippers.

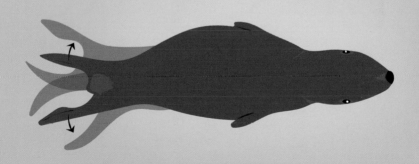

Seals swim using their hind flippers.

Pinniped Family Tree

The group pinniped includes seals, sea lions, and walrus.

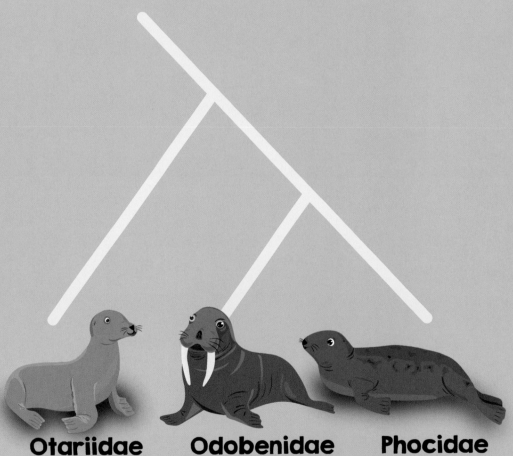

Otariidae
Fur Seals and
Sea Lions

Odobenidae
Walrus

Phocidae
Seal

16 species

1 species

19 species

Fur Seals
Are Not Seals!

The family Otariidae includes both fur seals and sea lions. True seals belong to the family Phocidae.

Don't confuse fur seals with the seals!

Anatomy of the Coccolithophore

(means "round stone bearer" in Latin)

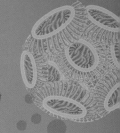

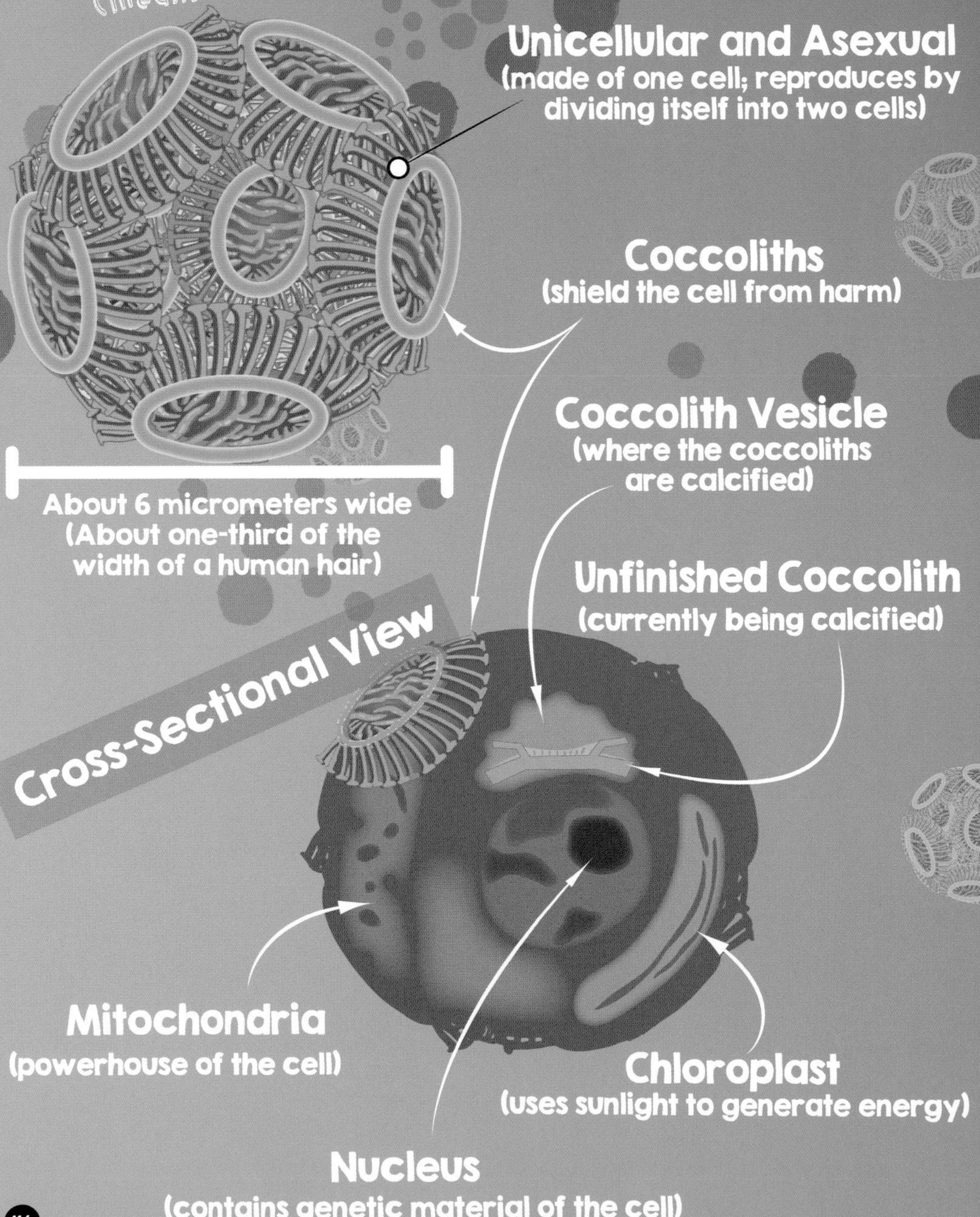
Unicellular and Asexual
(made of one cell; reproduces by dividing itself into two cells)
Coccoliths
(shield the cell from harm)
Coccolith Vesicle
(where the coccoliths are calcified)
About 6 micrometers wide
(About one-third of the width of a human hair)
Unfinished Coccolith
(currently being calcified)
Cross-Sectional View
Mitochondria
(powerhouse of the cell)
Chloroplast
(uses sunlight to generate energy)
Nucleus
(contains genetic material of the cell)

Protective Shields

Coccolithophores are microscopic unicellular phytoplankton that use photosynthesis (similar to plants). Though more research is needed, the coccoliths may provide protection from UV rays, grazers, and rough currents.

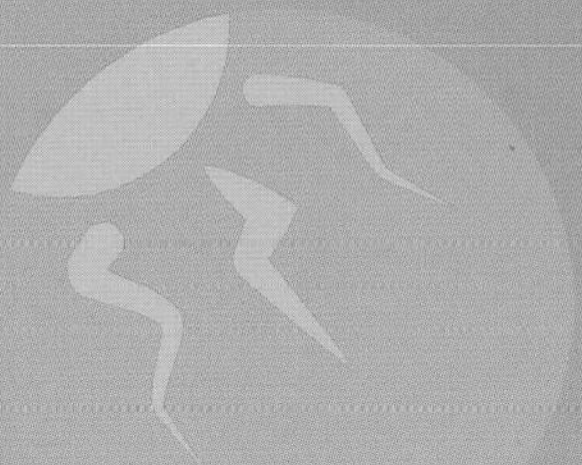

Ultraviolet Rays

Zooplankton

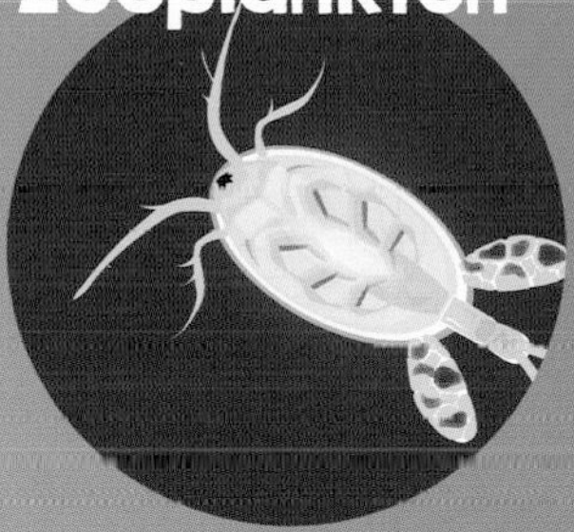

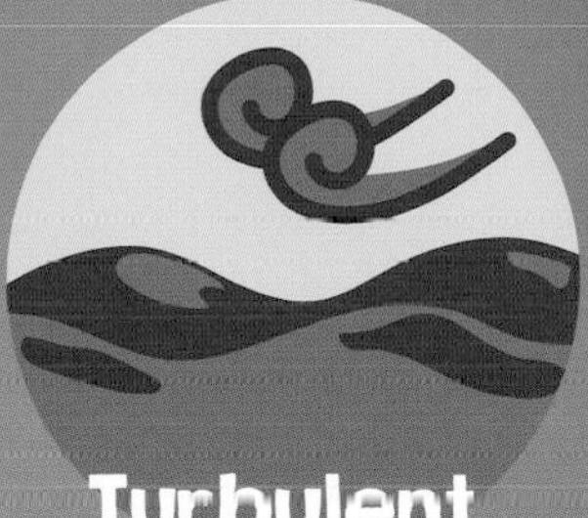

Turbulent Water Currents

Turning CO_2 Into Chalk

When coccolithophores die, they sink and carry the absorbed CO_2 to the deeper ocean. Tectonic movement, however, has lifted coccolithophores that sank 65 million years ago, forming the White Cliffs of Dover.

Psst, they're in England

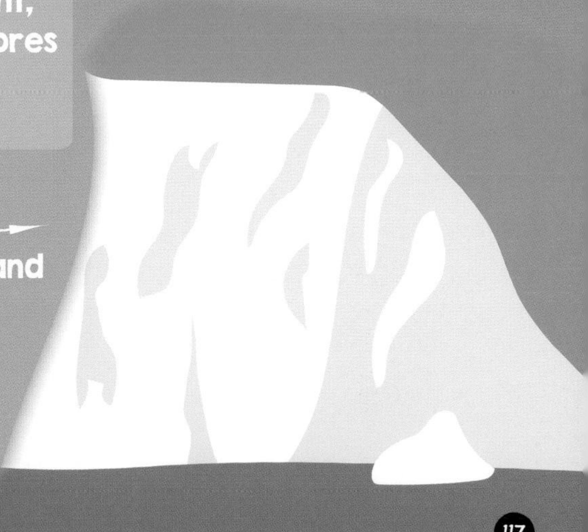

ANATOMY OF THE California Mantis Shrimp

(not a true shrimp, but still tastes great)

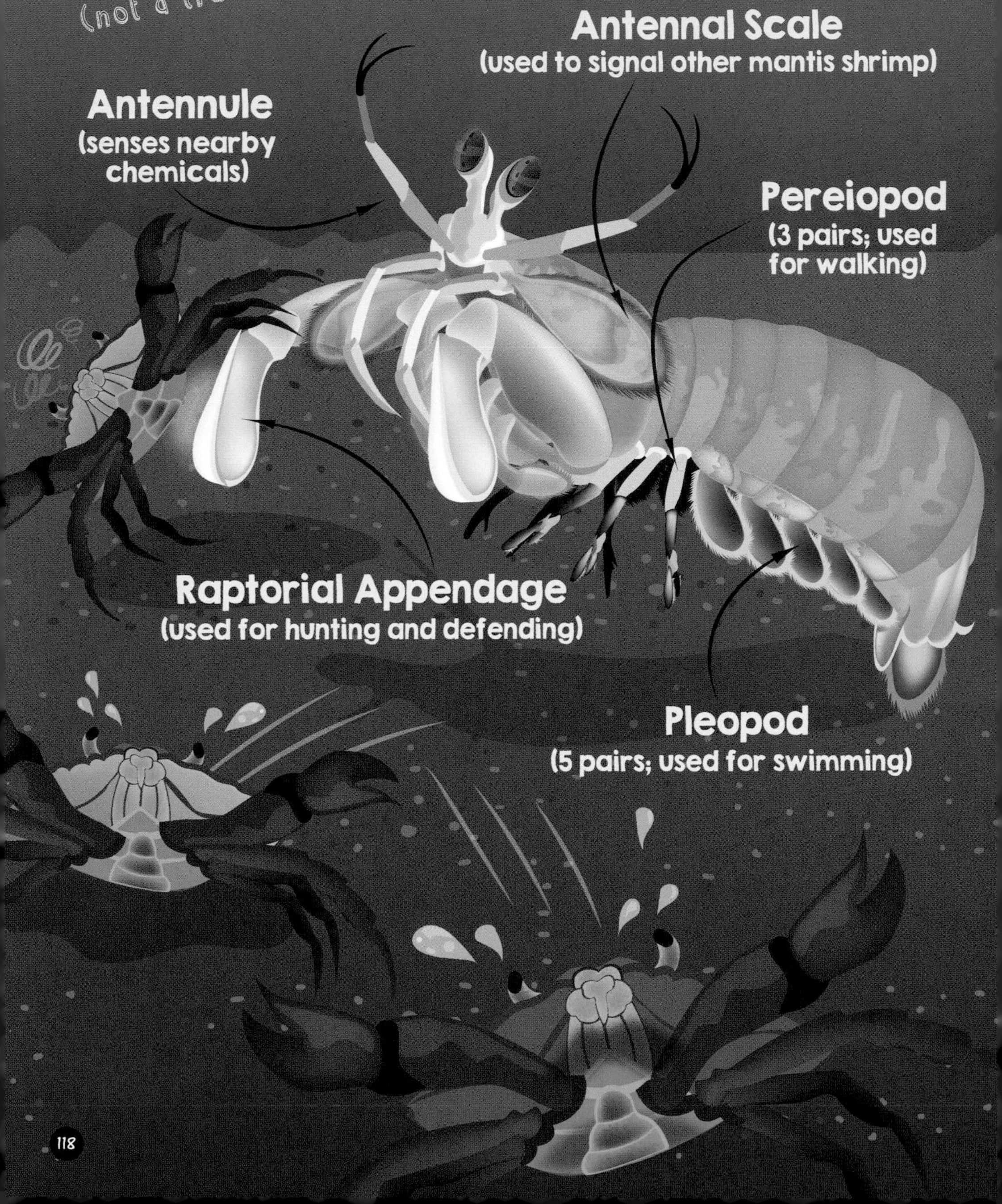
Antennal Scale
(used to signal other mantis shrimp)
Antennule
(senses nearby chemicals)
Pereiopod
(3 pairs; used for walking)
Raptorial Appendage
(used for hunting and defending)
Pleopod
(5 pairs; used for swimming)

Punching the Lights Out

The strike of the mantis shrimp only takes 4–8 milliseconds (nearly 100 times faster than an eyeblink)! The punch can form a cavitation bubble that implodes, generating forces that act as a second punch.

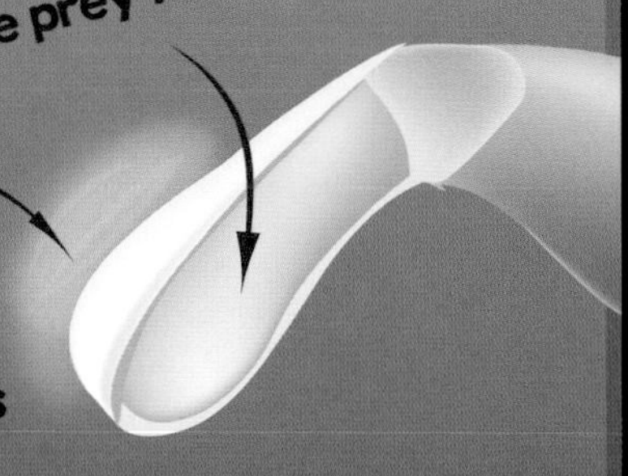

The punch hits the prey first.

Cavitation Bubble

Bubble implodes a few milliseconds later, striking the prey again.

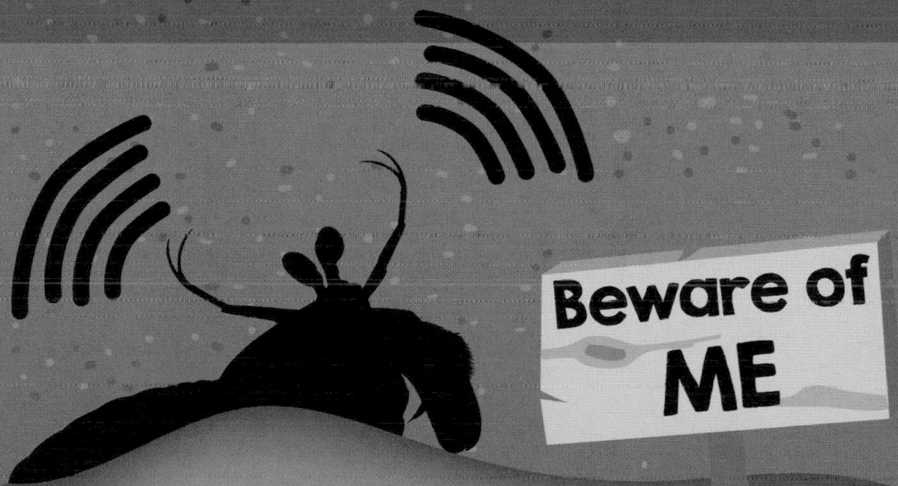
Beware of
ME

Warning Rumbles

A mantis shrimp can create low-frequency rumbles that travel long distances. This may serve as a mating call or to deter predators and competing mantis shrimp from coming closer.

Glossary

Ambience – the surrounding mood and noise; the vibe

Aquarists – people who maintain an aquarium

Calcified – hardened through the chemical association of calcium and carbonate

Camouflage – to blend in with the surroundings

Carcasses – the dead bodies of animals

Carnivorous – describes an animal that eats other animals for food

Chorion – a soft, permeable membrane that surrounds the developing embryo

Crustaceans – a group of animals from the phylum Arthropoda; common crustaceans include crabs, lobsters, crayfish, shrimp, and krill

Culling – selectively removing or killing off an unwanted animal

Ecosystem – a biological community including living animals and their nonliving habitat

Egg – female reproductive cell; creates a new organism when joined with a sperm

Embryos – developing animals; organisms that have not yet hatched

Extinction – the point at which every member of a species has died

Fertilization – the fusion of sperm and eggs to produce offspring

Filamentous – made up of thin threads

Finning – the practice of removing fins from an animal (often a shark) in order to sell the fins, leaving the animal to die

Herbicide – similar to pesticide, used to destroy unwanted plants such as weeds

IUCN – the International Union for the Conservation of Nature (IUCN) is an international organization that promotes sustainable use of natural resources

Kelp – a type of marine algae; often has gas-filled bladders and bladelike leaves

Krill – small, shrimplike crustacean (related to but not a shrimp)

Larval – describes a distinct preadult life stage

Metabolize – to perform metabolism (the series of chemical changes through which energy is processed to sustain life)

Mortality – another word for death

Natal – related to one's birth (a salmon's natal waters are the waters where it was born)

Neap Tide – period with the least difference between high and low tide

Nearsightedness – a condition of being able to see things that are near more clearly than things that are far away

Organism – an animal, plant, or single-cell life-form

pH – a number between 0 and 14 that indicates whether a chemical is an acid or a base

Photosynthesis – biological process that converts sunlight and carbon dioxide into glucose (energy) and oxygen

Phytoplankton – photosynthetic plankton

Pigments – biological material responsible for an organism's natural color

Plankton – small organisms that cannot swim against the currents

Poaching – the illegal taking and/or killing of an animal

Pollutant – a harmful chemical

Predators – animals that prey on other living organisms for food

Replicate – to repeat exactly

Saline – of high salt content; salty

Scavengers – animals that primarily prey on dead organisms

Secretes – produces, generates, or releases

Spawn – to be ready to mate and release sperm or eggs

Sperm – male reproductive cell; creates a new organism when joined with an egg

Spring Tide – period with the most difference between high and low tide

Symbiodinium – algae that commonly live within corals

Symbiotic – describes a cooperative relationship in which two or more organisms depend on one another for survival

Terrestrial – living on land

µM – a micromolar (µM) is a unit describing a concentration of one millionth of a mole per liter of solution

Unicellular – composed of only one cell

UV Rays – short for ultraviolet; invisible to the eye and responsible for sunburns

List of Sources

Anatomy of the Weedy Seadragon and Gimme Babies or Gimme Death!
1. Personal communication with Leslee Matsushige, Birch Aquarium, and Dr. Josefin Stiller, Scripps Institution of Oceanography.
2. Rouse, G.W., Stiller, J., Wilson, N.G. (2017) First live records of the ruby seadragon (*Phyllopteryx dewysea*, Syngnathidae). *Marine Biodiversity Records*. 10: 2.

Anatomy of the Coho Salmon
1. Fleming, I., Gross, M. (1994) Breeding competition in a Pacific salmon (Coho: *Oncorhynchus kisutch*): Measures of natural and sexual selection. *Evolution*. 48(3): 637–657.
2. Reimchen, T.E., et al. (2002) Isotopic evidence for enrichment of salmon-derived nutrients in vegetation, soil, and insects in riparian zones in coastal British Columbia. American Fishery Society Symposium.

The Life Cycle of the Sockeye Salmon
1. Groot, C., Margolis, L., Clarke, W.C. (1995) *Physiological ecology of Pacific salmon*. Vancouver, BC: UBC Press.
2. Whitney, C.K., Hinch, S.G., Patterson, D.A. (2014) Population origin and water temperature affect development timing in embryonic sockeye salmon. *Transactions of the American Fisheries Society*. 143(5): 1316–1329.
3. Folmar, L.C., Dickhoff, W.W. (1980) The parr—Smolt transformation (smoltification) and seawater adaptation in salmonids: A review of selected literature. *Aquaculture*. 21(1): 1–37.
4. Groot, C., Margolis, L. (1991) *Pacific salmon life histories*. Vancouver, BC: UBC Press.
5. Brown, R.S., et al. (2012) Quantifying mortal injury of juvenile Chinook salmon exposed to simulated hydro-turbine passage. *Transactions of the American Fisheries Society*. 141(1): 147–157.
6. Price, M.H., et al. (2011) Sea louse infection of juvenile sockeye salmon in relation to marine salmon farms on Canada's West Coast. *PLOS ONE*. 6(2): e16851.
7. Christensen, V., Trites, A.W. (2011) Predation on Fraser River sockeye salmon. *Cohen Commission Technical Report*. 8: 1–129. Vancouver, BC. www.cohencommission.ca
8. Craig, J.K., Foote, C.J. (2001) Countergradient variation and secondary sexual color: Phenotypic convergence promotes genetic divergence in carotenoid use between sympatric anadromous and nonanadromous morphs of sockeye salmon (*Oncorhynchus nerka*). *Evolution*. 55(2): 380–391.
9. Rand, P.S., et al. (2006) Effects of river discharge, temperature, and future climates on energetics and mortality of adult migrating Fraser River sockeye salmon. *Transactions of the American Fisheries Society*. 135(3): 655–667.
10. Burnett, N.J., et al. (2014) Burst swimming in areas of high flow: Delayed consequences of anaerobiosis in wild adult sockeye salmon. *Physiological and Biochemical Zoology*. 87(5): 587–598.
11. Reimchen, T.E., et al. (2002) Isotopic evidence for enrichment of salmon-derived nutrients in vegetation, soil, and insects in riparian zones in coastal British Columbia. American Fishery Society Symposium.
12. Battin, J., et al. (2007) Projected impacts of climate change on salmon habitat restoration. *PNAS*. 104(16): 6720–6725.

Anatomy of the Osedax
1. Katz, S., Rouse, G.W. (2013) The reproductive system of *Osedax* (Annelida, Siboglinidae): Ovary structure, sperm ultrastructure, and fertilization mode. *Invertebrate Biology*. 132: 368–385.
2. Rouse, G.W., Wilson, N.G., Worsaae, K., Vrijenhoek, R.C. (2015) A dwarf male reversal in bone-eating worms. *Current Biology*. 25(2): 236–241.

3. Rouse, G.W., Worsaae, K., Johnson, S.B., et al. (2008) Acquisition of dwarf male "harems" by recently settled females of *Osedax roseus* n. sp. (Siboglinidae; Annelida). *The Biological Bulletin*. 214: 67–82.
4. Tresguerres, M., Katz, S., Rouse, G.W. (2013) How to get into bones: Proton pump and carbonic anhydrase in *Osedax* boneworms. *Proceedings of the Royal Society B: Biological Sciences*. 280(1761): 20130625.
5. Worsaae, K., Rouse, G.W. (2010) The simplicity of males: Dwarf males of four species of *Osedax* (Siboglinidae; Annelida) investigated by confocal laser scanning microscopy. *Journal of Morphology*. 271: 127–142.

Anatomy of the Market Squid

1. Zeidberg, L.D., Butler, J.L., Ramon, D., Cossio, A., Stierhoff, K.L., Henry, A. (2011) Estimation of spawning habitats of market squid (*Doryteuthis opalescens*) from field surveys of eggs off Central and Southern California. *Marine Ecology*. 33: 326–336.
2. Kaufman, M.R., Ikeda, Y., Patton, C., van Dykhuizen, G., Epel, D. (1998) Bacterial symbionts colonize the accessory nidamental gland of the squid *Loligo opalescens* via horizontal transmission. *The Biological Bulletin*. 194: 36–43.
3. Biggs, J., Epel, D. (1991) Egg capsule sheath of *Loligo opalescens* Berry: Structure and association with bacteria. *Journal of Experimental Zoology*. 259: 263–267.

Market Squid Embryos Can Handle Stress, Yo

1. Navarro, M.O., Kwan, G.T., Batalov, O., Choi, C.Y., Pierce, N.T., Levin, L.A. (2016) Development of embryonic market squid, *Doryteuthis opalescens*, under chronic exposure to low environmental pH and [O_2]. *PLOS ONE* 11: e0167461.
2. Fields, W.G. (1965) The structure, development, food relations, reproduction, and life history of the squid, *Loligo opalescens*, Berry. *CA Fish Bulletin*. 131: 1–105.

Anatomy of the Bluefin Tuna

1. Carey, F.G., Teal, J.M. (1969) Regulation of body temperature by the bluefin tuna. *Comparative Biochemistry and Physiology*. 28: 205–213.
2. Storelli, M.M. (2008) Potential human health risks from metals (Hg, Cd, and Pb) and polychlorinated biphenyls (PCBs) via seafood consumption: Estimation of target hazard quotients (THQs) and toxic equivalents (TEQs). *Food and Chemical Toxicology*. 46: 2782–2788.
3. Downs, S.G., MacLeod, C.L., Lester, J.N. (1998) Mercury in precipitation and its relation to bioaccumulation in fish: A literature review. *Water, Air, and Soil Pollution*. 108(1-2): 149–187.

Anatomy of the California Grunion

1. Griem, J.N., Martin, K.L.M. (2000) Wave action: The environmental trigger for hatching in the California grunion *Leuresthes tenuis* (Teleostei: Atherinopsidae). *Marine Biology*. 137: 177–181.

Anatomy of the Horseshoe Crab

1. Novitsky, T.J. (2009) Biomedical applications of *Limulus* amebocyte lysate. In *Biology and conservation of horseshoe crabs*, pp. 315–329. Boston, MA: Springer.
2. Brusca, R.C., Brusca, G.J. (2003) *Invertebrates*. Sunderland, MA: Sinauer Associates.
3. Battelle, B.A. (2016) Simple eyes, extraocular photoreceptors and opsins in the American horseshoe crab. *Integrative and Comparative Biology*. 56(5): 809–819.

Anatomy of the Yeti Crab

1. Goffredi, S.K., Jones, W.J., Erhlich, H., Springer, A., Vrijenhoek, R.C. (2008) Epibiotic bacteria associated with the recently discovered yeti crab, *Kiwa hirsuta*. *Environmental Microbiology*. 10(10): 2623–2634.
2. Macpherson, E., Jones, W., Segonzac, M. (2005) A new squat lobster family of Galatheoidea (Crustacea, Decapoda, Anomura) from the hydrothermal vents of the Pacific-Antarctic Ridge. *Zoosystema*. 27: 709–723.
3. Thurber, A.R., Jones, W.J., Schnabel, K. (2011) Dancing for food in the deep sea: Bacterial farming by a new species of yeti crab. *PLOS ONE*. 6(11): e26243.

Anatomy of the Tuna Crab

1. Boyd, C.M. (1967) The benthic and pelagic habitats of the red crab, *Pleuroncodes planipes*. *Pacific Science*. 21: 394–403.
2. Aurioles-Gamboa, D. (1992) Inshore-offshore movements of pelagic red crabs *Pleuroncodes planipes* (Decapoda, Anomura, Galatheidae) off the Pacific coast of Baja California Sur, Mexico. *Crustaceana*. 62: 71–84.
3. Alverson, F.G. (1963) The food of yellowfin and skipjack tunas in the Eastern Tropical Pacific Ocean. *Inter-American Tropical Tuna Commission Bulletin*. 7(5): 293–396.

The Fallacy of Sharks

1. Deadliest Animals: http://www.gatesnotes.com/health/most-lethal-animal-mosquito-week
2. Global Shark Statistics: https://www.flmnh.ufl.edu/fish/sharks/statistics/statsw.htm
3. Worm, B., et al. (2013) Global catches, exploitation rates, and rebuilding options for sharks. *Marine Policy*. 40: 194–294.

Anatomy of the Giant Manta Ray

1. The Manta Trust. www.mantatrust.org.

Anatomy of the Swell Shark

1. Gruber, D.F., Loew, E.R., Deheyn, D.D., Akkaynak, D., Gaffney, J.P., Smith, W.L., et al. (2016) Biofluorescence in catsharks (Scyliorhinidae): Fundamental description and relevance for elasmobranch visual ecology. *Scientific Reports*. 6: 24751.

Sharktunes

1. Nosal, A.P., Keenan, E.A., Hastings, P.A., Gneezy, A. (2016) The effect of background music in shark documentaries on viewers' perceptions of sharks. *PLOS ONE*. 11(8): e0159279. https://doi.org/10.1371/journal.pone.0159279

Anatomy of the Moon Jelly

1. Trujillo, A., Thurman, H. (2013) *Essentials of oceanography*. Boston, MA: Pearson.
2. Holstein, T., Tardent, P. (1984) An ultrahigh-speed analysis of exocytosis: Nematocyst discharge. *Science*. 223: 830–833.

Anatomy of the *Velella velella*

1. Brusca, R.C., Brusca, G.J. (2003) *Invertebrates*. Sunderland, MA: Sinauer Associates.

Anatomy of the Green Sea Turtle

1. Brothers, J.R., Lohmann, K.J. (2015) Evidence for geomagnetic imprinting and magnetic navigation in the natal homing of sea turtles. *Current Biology*. 25: 392–396.
2. Lohmann, K.J., Lohmann, C.M.F., Brothers, J.R., Putman, N.F. (2013) Natal homing and imprinting in sea turtles. In *The biology of sea turtles*, volume III, pp. 59–77. Boca Raton, FL: CRC Press.
3. Witherington, B., Hirama, S., Hardy, R. (2012) Young sea turtles of the pelagic *Sargassum*-dominated drift community: Habitat use, population density, and threats. *Marine Ecology Progress Series*. 463: 1–22.

Anatomy of the Narwhal

1. Laidre, K.L., Heide-Jørgensen, M.P. (2005) Winter feeding intensity of narwhals (*Monodon monoceros*). *Marine Mammal Science*. 21: 45–57.
2. Nweeia, M.T., Eichmiller, F.C., Hauschka, P.V., Donahue, G.A., Orr, J.R., Ferguson, S.H., Watt, C.A., Mead, J.G., Potter, C.W., Dietz, R., Giuseppetti, A.A., Black, S.R., Trachtenberg, A.J., Kuo, W.P. (2014) Sensory ability in the narwhal tooth organ system. *The Anatomical Record*. 297: 599–617.
3. Ravetch, A. (May 12, 2017). How narwhals use their tusks. World Wildlife Fund. https://www.worldwildlife.org/videos/how-narwhals-use-their-tusks

Anatomy of the Leptocephalus

1. Tesch, F.W., White, R.J. (2003) *The eel*. Oxford, UK: Blackwell Publishing.
2. Fahay, M.P. (1983) Guide to the early stages of marine fishes occurring in the western North Atlantic Ocean, Cape Hatteras to the southern Scotian Shelf. *Journal of Northwest Atlantic Fishery Science*. 4: 58–59.
3. Hulet, W.H., Robins, C.R. (1989) The evolutionary significance of the leptocephalus larva. In *Fishes of the Western North Atlantic*. Leptocephali. Part 9, vol 2, pp. 669–677. New Haven, CT: Sears Foundation for Marine Research.

Anatomy of the Coral Polyp

1. Brown, B.E., Bythell, J.C. (2005) Perspectives on mucus secretion in reef corals. *Marine Ecology Progress Series*. 296: 291–309.
2. Baker, A. (2003) Flexibility and specificity in coral-algal symbiosis: Diversity, ecology, and biogeography of *Symbiodinium*. *Annual Review of Ecology, Evolution, and Systematics*. 34: 661–689.

Sea Lions vs. Seals

1. Berta, A., Sumich, J.L., Kovacs, K.M. (2005) *Marine mammals, second edition: Evolutionary biology*. Burlington, MA: Academic Press.
2. Boness, D.J. (2002) Sea lions: Overview. In Perrin, W.F., Würsig, B., Thewissen, J.G.M. (Eds.) *Encyclopedia of Marine Mammals*, pp. 998–1001. Burlington, MA: Elsevier. Web.

Anatomy of the Coccolithophore

1. Young, J.R. (1994) Functions of coccoliths. In Winter, A., Siesser, W.G. (Eds.) *Coccolithophores*, pp. 63–82. Cambridge: Cambridge University Press.
2. Moheimani, N.R., Webb, J.P., Borowitzka, M.A. (2012) Bioremediation and other potential applications of coccolithophorid algae: A review. *Algal Research*. 1(2): 120–133.
3. Jordan, R.W. (2012) Haptophyta. In *eLS*. Chichester, UK: John Wiley & Sons, Ltd.

Anatomy of the California Mantis Shrimp

1. Burrows, M. (1969) The mechanics and neural control of the prey capture strike in the mantid shrimps *Squilla* and *Hemisquilla*. *Z. vergl. Physiologie*. 62: 361–381.
2. Patek, S.N., Rosario, M.V., Taylor, J.R.A. (2013) Comparative spring mechanics in mantis shrimp. *The Journal of Experimental Biology*. 216: 1317–1329.
3. Staaterman, E.R., Clark, C.W., Gallagher, A.J., deVries, M.S., Claverie, T., Patek, S.N. (2011) Rumbling in the benthos: Acoustic ecology of the California mantis shrimp *Hemisquilla californiensis*. *Aquatic Biology*. 13: 97–105.

About Squidtoons

Since 2013, Squidtoons has been translating scientific research into engaging illustrations in order to connect the public and the scientific community. Our goal is to create informative comics without sacrificing scientific accuracy. Much like scientific writing, our work is created by a scientific team and reviewed by multiple experts before it is published. We hope you enjoy it!

About the Authors

Garfield Kwan is a PhD candidate studying marine fish physiology at the Scripps Institution of Oceanography at the University of California San Diego. Originally from Hong Kong, Garfield moved to California at the age of eight. The founder and director of Squidtoons, Garfield works with researchers across the country to make science enjoyable, accessible, and accurate.

Dana Song graduated from the University of California San Diego in 2016 with a degree in public health. Originally from Phelan, California, Dana spends her time mountain biking and creating digital illustrations for Squidtoons.